An Instant Guide to
SMALL PETS

*A complete guide to the wide range of
small pets, from the most common to the exotic,
described and illustrated in full color*

WRITTEN AND ILLUSTRATED BY
CECILIA FITZSIMONS

GRAMERCY BOOKS
NEW YORK

Dedicated to Mamy and Papou, Paulette and François Baudin,
for the gift of their friendship.

With special thanks to Liz Baker VN.

 CAUTION

Many pet animals have the ability to cause injury to their owners:
cats can scratch; rabbits can kick; dogs, cats, rodents, parrots (large
and small) and many reptiles can bite. Most will do so only if they
feel threatened, so do not tease your pet or handle it roughly. Do
not get too close to an animal you do not know unless the owner
says it is safe to do so.

Within the book, this symbol ! appears against the very few
animals that may need to be treated with special caution.
See also the section on hygiene and safety on page 19.

PLEASE NOTE

**IT IS ILLEGAL TO BUY ANY ENDANGERED OR RARE SPECIES CAPTURED FROM THE
WILD. ALWAYS BUY ANIMALS THAT HAVE BEEN BRED IN CAPTIVITY.**

This 2000 edition is published by Gramercy Books™,
an imprint of Random House Value Publishing, Inc.,
201 East 50th Street, New York, New York 10022.

Gramercy Books™ and colophon are trademarks of
Random House Value Publishing, Inc.

Random House
New York • Toronto • London • Sydney • Auckland
http://www.randomhouse.com/

Printed and bound in Malaysia

A CIP catalog record for this book is available
from the Library of Congress.

ISBN 0-517-20873-3
8 7 6 5 4 3 2 1

Contents

Introduction

Human beings are not solitary creatures and the keeping and caring of a pet is something that seems to be quite fundamental to human nature. Until a hundred years ago, animals were a part of everyday life – used for transportation, as beasts of burden, to assist with hunting, herding, and pest control, and, finally, for companionship. Even today, at least half the households in Europe and North America have a pet of one sort or another.

Many types of animal are now available as pets. This book describes the most common small pets and gives a brief description of their requirements in terms of the accommodation, feeding, attention and veterinary care that you must give them. Having selected a pet you will then need to obtain further, more detailed care information from your veterinarian, pet breeder and specialist books.

The happiest, healthiest pets are those kept in conditions that most closely resemble the ones their wild relatives enjoy. Provide living quarters large enough for active life and a specially prepared quality commercial food. Exercise, fresh air and a supplement of natural, fresh foods keep animals fit and help to alleviate boredom. Allow as much freedom as possible in the yard or inside your home – but always make sure that your pet is secure and cannot escape or injure itself. Isolate electric cables, poisonous plants and deep water; close windows and doors, cover windows and mirrors (birds), block chimneys and other escape routes; turn off cooking appliances, fans or anything else that might cause injury. Make sure cats and dogs cannot reach smaller prey animals such as birds, fish and mice.

How to use this book

The book is divided into five sections – one for each of the major groups of pet animals that are readily available. A different color band at the top of the page identifies each section.

MAMMALS	includes small dogs, cats, rabbits, guinea pigs, mice and rats, hamsters, chinchillas and ferrets
BIRDS	includes parakeets, parrots, canaries, other finches, pigeons and miscellaneous species
FISH	includes tropical and coldwater species
REPTILES and AMPHIBIA	includes tortoises, turtles, lizards, snakes, frogs, toads newts and salamanders
INVERTEBRATES	includes insects, spiders and snails

On every page, one of the following symbols appears in the section colour band to identify the type of animal more precisely.

 SMALL DOGS – wolf-like carnivores; social pack animals.

 CATS – nocturnal hunters, retractile claws, whiskers.

 RABBITS – lagomorphs; long ears, long hind legs, short fluffy tail.

 GUINEA PIGS – short-bodied rodents, no tail, gnawing teeth.

 MICE AND RATS pointed-nosed rodents, long non-furry tail.

 HAMSTERS – small rodents, cheeks with pouches, short tail.

 GERBILS – small desert rodents, furry tail, long hind legs.

 CHIPMUNK – small, squirrel-like rodent.

 CHINCHILLA – short-bodied rodent, hairy tail, very soft fur.

 FERRET – weasel-like carnivore, long thin body.

 BUDGERIGARS – small parrots (also popularly known as Parakeets).

 PARROTS – hooked beak with fleshy cere at base, clasping claws.

 CANARIES – brightly colored finches, short beak for seed-eating.

 OTHER FINCHES – seed eaters, perching feet.

 PIGEONS – medium size, short beak with fleshy cere at base.

 OTHER BIRDS – various species.

 TROPICAL FISH – mostly freshwater fish from tropical regions.

 COLDWATER FISH freshwater fish from cool temperate regions.

 TORTOISES / TURTLES reptiles with a bony shell.

 LIZARDS – long scaly bodied reptiles; usually live in hot dry regions.

 SNAKES – legless reptiles, elongated scaly body; sinuous movement.

 AMPHIBIA – scaleless moist skin; aquatic larvae, most adults terrestrial.

 INVERTEBRATES – soft-bodied animals without backbones.

 Denotes an animal that may need to be treated with caution.

9

Specimen page

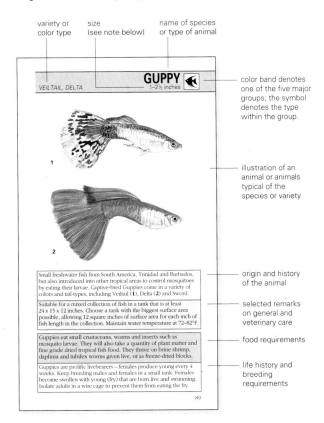

variety or color type

size (see note below)

name of species or type of animal

VEILTAIL, DELTA

1–2½ inches

color band denotes one of the five major groups; the symbol denotes the type within the group.

illustration of an animal or animals typical of the species or variety

1

2

Small freshwater fish from South America, Trinidad and Barbados, but also introduced into other tropical areas to control mosquitoes by eating their larvae. Captive-bred Guppies come in a variety of colors and tail-types, including Veiltail (**1**), Delta (**2**) and Sword.

origin and history of the animal

Suitable for a mixed collection of fish in a tank that is at least 24 x 15 x 12 inches. Choose a tank with the biggest surface area possible, allowing 12 square inches of surface area for each inch of fish length in the collection. Maintain water temperature at 72–82°F.

selected remarks on general and veterinary care

Guppies eat small crustaceans, worms and insects such as mosquito larvae. They will also take a quantity of plant matter and fine grade dried tropical fish food. They thrive on brine shrimp, daphnia and tubifex worms given live, or as freeze-dried blocks.

food requirements

Guppies are prolific livebearers – females produce young every 4 weeks. Keep breeding males and females in a small tank. Females become swollen with young (fry) that are born live and swimming. Isolate adults in a wire cage to prevent them from eating the fry.

life history and breeding requirements

89

Notes

When several pages describe varieties of the same type of animal, as in rabbits, the bottom three boxes give information for the whole species.

Size of animals – weight, or the length from the tip of the nose to the end of the tail, except for dogs where the measurement is the height from the top of the shoulder to the ground.

Size of accommodation – throughout this book the size of cages, runs, tanks and so on, is given as length x height x width – as if the cage or tank is viewed from the front.

Selecting a pet

Careful consideration must be given to the selection of a pet. You must choose an animal that fits in with your lifestyle and that will be happy with the home and care you are able to provide. Whenever possible you should provide your pet with living conditions that mimic its natural environment. The conditions of temperature, comfort, food and mental stimulation should all resemble those experienced by wild members of the same species.

Pedigree or crossbreeds?

Pedigree animals are more expensive than crossbreeds but if you want a particular color or type then a pedigree may be the answer. Crossbreeds are just as loving and may be less prone to some medical problems caused by in-breeding. Remember that a young animal may give you little idea of what its adult size and temperament will be.

Accommodation

The more space your pet has to move around in the happier it will be. The measurements for cage and tank sizes given in this book are the smallest required for each species but always try to provide something larger. Have the accommodation ready before you bring your new pet home. Do not fuss with it too much at first; leave it alone so that it can quietly get used to its new surroundings.

Costs

Make a list of the costs you will incur. Add up the cost of the pet, its accommodation and equipment, and weekly food and bedding. Also include the cost of inoculations, neutering and other likely vet bills. Insurance policies are available to cover veterinary fees. Finally, you must consider the cost in terms of your spare time. How long will it take to exercise your pet, feed it, clean out its cage and so on? Can you spare this amount of time every day?

The pet

Each pet has its own particular requirements. If you and your family are out all day will the pet need company while you are away? Dogs, obviously, need exercise – at least three times a day. Other animals need exercise too. Rabbits, tortoises, chinchillas, and guinea pigs should be exercised in an enclosed run in the yard. If possible, birds should be allowed free flight in the house (see page 8) or an aviary. Hamsters and mice need an exercise wheel. Cats are free ranging, but should you keep a cat if you live near a busy road?

Finally, is your new pet going to be acceptable to the other members of your family? Some people are allergic to cats and other animals. Others are absolutely terrified of certain animals – spiders and snakes in particular. Will any other pet that you may already have get along with the new arrival? Be especially careful to separate predator pets (cats, dogs, ferrets) from prey animals (rabbits, guinea pigs, mice, birds, and fish).

Housing your pet

Dog

Most dogs live free within the home and need little more than a warm place to sleep. They should not be encouraged to sleep on beds and other furniture, so provide a dog bed in a quiet corner where the animal will not be disturbed. If the dog is allowed to run free in the yard make sure that the fences are high enough and without holes so that they cannot escape. A dog-door fitted to an external door allows easy access in and out of the house for small dogs.

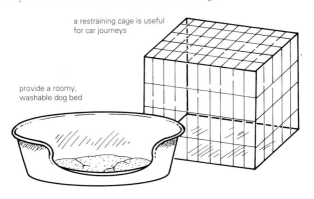

a restraining cage is useful for car journeys

provide a roomy, washable dog bed

Cat

Provide a washable cat bed – cats particularly like to sleep in an enclosed space, try a cat nest or cardboard box. Most cats are free-ranging; a cat-door fitted to an external door enables the animal to follow its nocturnal hunting instincts at night. If kept indoors, even overnight, provide cat litter in a shallow tray.

a scratching pole may help to divert your cat away from your furniture – but don't rely on it

carry in a secure pet carrier when traveling

cat nest

cat litter box

Outdoor hutch and run

Wooden hutch

A large wooden hutch can be kept outside provided it is covered with weatherproof material such as roofing felt. Fix firmly in a position that is sheltered from the wind and shaded from the sun in hot weather. Suitable for guinea pigs, chinchillas and ferrets in summer, and rabbits all the year. Guinea pigs and chinchillas can become ill following the shock of sudden changes of temperature, so avoid moving them between the house and the yard in cold or very hot weather

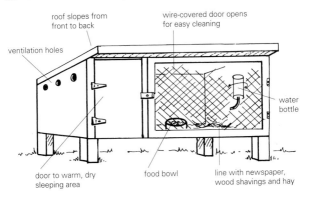

roof slopes from front to back

wire-covered door opens for easy cleaning

ventilation holes

water bottle

door to warm, dry sleeping area

food bowl

line with newspaper, wood shavings and hay

Run

A wooden-framed, wire-covered run provides a safe exercise area for rabbits, guinea pigs and tortoises in good weather. Move around the lawn to provide fresh grass to eat. Check that rabbits are not digging escape burrows. Provide shade and drinking water in summer.

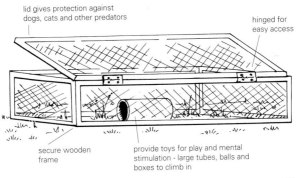

lid gives protection against dogs, cats and other predators

hinged for easy access

secure wooden frame

provide toys for play and mental stimulation - large tubes, balls and boxes to climb in

Small indoor cages

Mice, rats, hamsters and gerbils can be kept in a metal cage with a heavy duty plastic base.

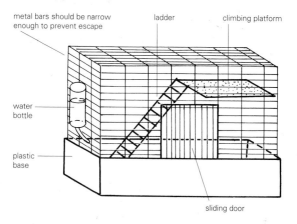

metal bars should be narrow enough to prevent escape

ladder

climbing platform

water bottle

plastic base

sliding door

Plastic tube systems

These provide a great variety of tunnels, and chambers that can be linked to a central terrarium.

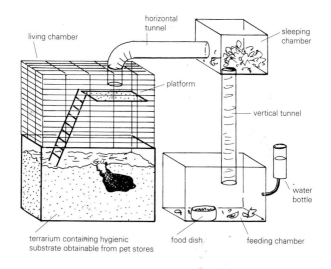

living chamber

horizontal tunnel

sleeping chamber

platform

vertical tunnel

water bottle

terrarium containing hygienic substrate obtainable from pet stores

food dish

feeding chamber

Large indoor cage

Large cages with heavy-duty wire are ideal homes for chipmunks, chinchillas, house rabbits, guinea pigs and ferrets. Similar, tall cages are used for parrots and other cage birds. Choose a cage with a metal or heavy-duty plastic base. Depending on the pet, line with newspaper, a deep layer of wood shavings or peat to burrow in, or grit. Wire-bottomed cages, as used in fur farms to keep chinchillas and Angora rabbits clean, may lead to sore feet; line with heavy-duty plastic sheeting and then cover with a suitable substrate.

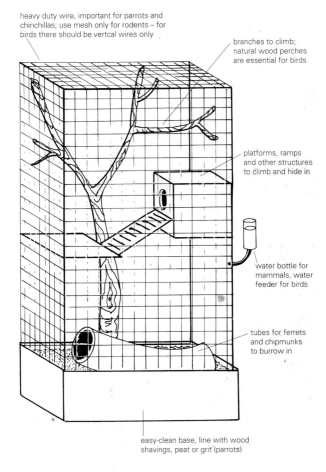

heavy duty wire, important for parrots and chinchillas; use mesh only for rodents – for birds there should be vertical wires only

branches to climb; natural wood perches are essential for birds

platforms, ramps and other structures to climb and hide in

water bottle for mammals, water feeder for birds

tubes for ferrets and chipmunks to burrow in

easy-clean base, line with wood shavings, peat or grit (parrots)

Bird cages

Box cage

Bird cages for indoor use are either open (see large indoor cage) or enclosed – a box cage. A box cage is made of wood or metal and is enclosed on the top, sides and back. This type of cage is popularly used for finches, in particular.

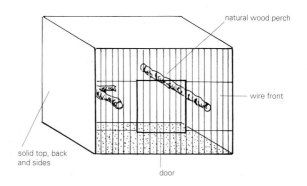

natural wood perch

wire front

solid top, back
and sides

door

Aviary

If you have space, a large outdoor aviary can accommodate a collection of different birds. In cool climates provide a wooden, shed-like shelter. This should be insulated and heated in winter if tropical birds are kept.

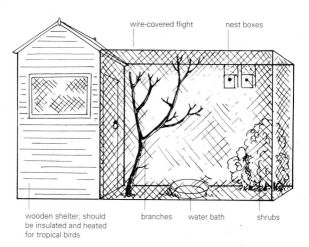

wire-covered flight

nest boxes

wooden shelter; should
be insulated and heated
for tropical birds

branches   water bath   shrubs

Glass and plastic tanks

Glass cut to any size can be joined with silicone sealant to form tanks in a great variety of shapes. Plastic tanks with a close-fitting, ventilated lid are suitable for small pets

Aquarium
Filled with water, this is a tank for aquatic pets such as fish.

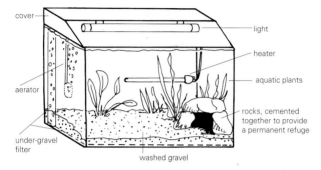

cover

light

heater

aquatic plants

aerator

rocks, cemented together to provide a permanent refuge

under-gravel filter

washed gravel

Terrarium
A tank used to recreate a terrestrial habitat for reptiles, amphibia, small rodents, and so on. A large tank, half-filled with woodshavings or peat, is an ideal, draft-free home for gerbils, rats and other small burrowing rodents. Fit with a ventilated lid that is escape- and cat-proof.

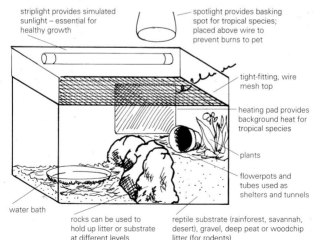

striplight provides simulated sunlight – essential for healthy growth

spotlight provides basking spot for tropical species; placed above wire to prevent burns to pet

tight-fitting, wire mesh top

heating pad provides background heat for tropical species

plants

flowerpots and tubes used as shelters and tunnels

water bath

rocks can be used to hold up litter or substrate at different levels

reptile substrate (rainforest, savannah, desert), gravel, deep peat or woodchip litter (for rodents)

Pet care

Good pet care is essential. It will prevent illness and your pet will be happier and will live longer.

Feeding

Pets should be fed regularly and at the same time(s). Most species are fed every day, but some, such as reptiles, are fed every few days. Place the food in a clean, heavy, earthenware bowl that will not tip over. All sizes are available, from large dog-sized to small mouse-sized. Wash bowls daily, and sterilize at least once a week in boiling water or in a dishwasher. Fresh water should be given daily. Water bottles and feeders are particularly suitable for small mammals and birds because they prevent spillage and keep the water clean. Bottles should be cleaned once a week with a bottle brush. Give a variety of good quality foods as recommended for each type of pet. Always check that commercially prepared foods are still within their "sell-by" date. Wash all fresh foods to remove pesticides and the possible infection from wild animals. Sterilize pieces of fruit-wood, used for chewing and perches, with boiling water.

Above all, do not overfeed any pet. Obesity causes serious health problems and will shorten a pet's life considerably. Give a moderate diet and plenty of exercise.

Cleaning out

This is the least popular aspect of keeping a pet. However, it must be done regularly as dirty living quarters always cause serious health problems. If an animal's living space is soiled and wet with droppings, it needs cleaning right away. Wash dog and cat beds and bedding regularly to prevent fleas breeding in the bed. Remove soiled cat litter from the box several times a day. Use a scraper and a stiff-bristled brush to remove soiled bedding from hutches and cages. Make sure that all the corners are clean, and spray with a mild animal cage disinfectant. Allow to dry thoroughly before lining the cage with paper and dust-free wood shavings. For rabbits, spread a layer of clean, fresh timothy hay on top. Do not use moldy hay, which can cause respiratory diseases, or straw, which may result in eye injuries and has little nutritional value anyway. Indoor metal and plastic cages should be washed thoroughly, disinfected and dried.

Depending on the species, part of the water in a fish tank should be replaced regularly with fresh, dechlorinated tap water. Remove the chlorine by allowing the water to stand overnight in a bucket or aerate vigorously for several hours. At least once a week, siphon up the food remains from the bottom of the tank and scrape algae from the glass. Check and clean filters regularly. If droppings are removed every day from a terrarium it will remain in good condition for some time. Eventually, though, the whole tank will have to be emptied, cleaned and the old substrate replaced with new.

Grooming

Regular grooming keeps your pet feeling comfortable and looking smart. Use a brush and comb to suit the animal. If a bath is necessary, use a little very mild shampoo in shallow, tepid water. Place a piece of towel in the bottom of the bath to prevent slipping. Rinse and dry well in a warm place. Birds need to bathe regularly to keep their feathers in good condition. Sprinkle a bird with water from a spray bottle in its cage, or let it splash in a shallow dish or in an enclosed bird bath attached to the cage door. Allow it to air-dry.

Veterinary care

Register your new pet with a local vet and take it along for a check up. The vet will advise you of the inoculations that will be needed and will neuter the animal if you do not wish to breed from it. At least once a week, give your pet a quick health check. Are the teeth, beak or claws in need of a trim? Claws often become overgrown in caged animals – reduce the need for clipping by providing plenty of exercise outside. Birds have similar problems if they are not given natural, irregular branches to perch on. Check the fur, feather and skin condition. Make sure that there are no signs of parasites. De-worm and treat for flea control regularly. Is your animal generally looking well? Not subdued, off its food or bad tempered? There should be no discharges from the eyes, mouth, ears or rear end. The droppings should not be runny or discolored.

Handling

Most pets should be handled and exercised daily; this gives them both physical and mental exercise and is an enjoyable experience for owners as well. If you are releasing the pet in the house, make sure that the room is secure, with no hidden escape routes up chimneys or under floorboards. Cover all electrical wires that could be chewed. Remove any poisonous houseplants. Handle your pet firmly and with confidence; if you are frightened the animal will sense it. If you don't know how to pick up your pet properly, ask your vet.

Hygiene and safety

Always wash your hands well after handling a pet. Some can carry infectious diseases – turtles (and many other reptiles), for example, carry salmonella. Pets rarely transmit diseases but care should be taken with members of the parrot family. Avoid contact with any wheezy birds; they can pass on a serious disease called psittacosis and other diseases. Most pet owners can expect a small scratch or bite from a pet at some time or other, but treat even the smallest scratch immediately because many animals carry a cocktail of germs on their teeth and claws. A few sensible precautions will avoid serious injuries. Do not separate fighting animals with your bare hands. Rabbits can kick powerfully enough to break their own backs; so hold them securely under their rear legs. Never put your fingers near a parrot's beak – it is designed to bite through hard wood and some of the hardest nuts in the world.

Common fur colors

Pets, especially mammals, are bred in a wide variety of colors. Some of the most common are shown below.

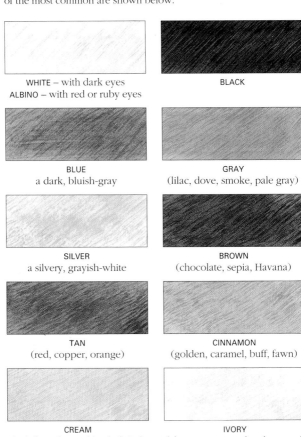

WHITE – with dark eyes
ALBINO – with red or ruby eyes

BLACK

BLUE
a dark, bluish-gray

GRAY
(lilac, dove, smoke, pale gray)

SILVER
a silvery, grayish-white

BROWN
(chocolate, sepia, Havana)

TAN
(red, copper, orange)

CINNAMON
(golden, caramel, buff, fawn)

CREAM
(pale fawn, honey, blonde, beige)

IVORY
(champagne, pearl, pale cream)

AGOUTI
normal ticked fur

CHINCHILLA
gray agouti

Common coat patterns

Breeders are continually striving to develop new coat patterns in their animals. The most common patterns are shown below.

SOLID-COLORED
all one color

HIMALAYAN
(Siamese, sealpoint)
resembles a Siamese cat

DUTCH
resembles a
Friesian cow

TORTOISESHELL
resembles a
tortoiseshell cat

BI-COLORED
two colors

TRI-COLORED
three colors

RUMPWHITE
has a white rump

BELTED or BANDED
has a white band
around the middle

VARIEGATED
(piebald, mosaic,
dalmatian, brindle)
mixed or spotted

THE DOG

6–32 inches (height at shoulder)

Domestic dogs, descended from the Gray Wolf, have lived and worked with human beings since prehistoric times some 12,000 years ago. Large and small dogs soon developed; by Roman times most of the major dog types could be recognized.

Provide a washable bed, groom, and treat for fleas and worms regularly. At 6 weeks, and annually, vaccinate against parvo virus, distemper, hepatitis, leptospirosis, and rabies. A vet will tattoo the dog's ear or insert a microchip to identify the animal if lost.

Dogs are omnivorous – they eat a wide variety of meat, vegetable and cereal foods, not just meat alone. Fresh, frozen, canned and dried foods may be given, but a "complete" dried food provides everything that a dog needs except water – give fresh daily.

To prevent unwanted puppies and mammary tumors, bitches should be spayed before their first season, and dogs neutered at 6 months. House-train a puppy, and teach to be obedient both on and off the lead. Give plenty of mental and physical exercise daily.

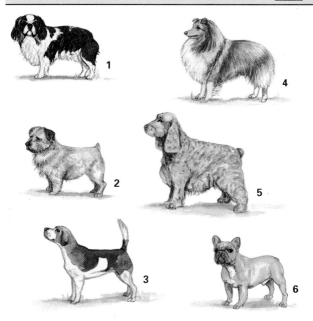

Breeds were developed to carry out various tasks and are still grouped on their ability to hunt, herd, guard, pull loads or act as companions

TOY DOGS are small, affectionate companions. They were bred as lap dogs for aristocratic ladies and gentlemen. They include the Papillon, Pekingese, Maltese and King Charles Spaniel (**1**).

TERRIERS are small, hunting dogs that were used to dig out rats and rabbits. Breeds such as the Norfolk Terrier (**2**) are named after the area in which they originated. Fox Terriers were used to hunt foxes.

HOUNDS are large hunting dogs. There are a few small hounds, including the Basset Hound, the Beagle (**3**) and Dachshunds.

HERDING DOGS are used to control sheep, cattle, reindeer or goats. Most of them are large, but the Shetland Sheepdog (**4**) and Welsh Corgi are small.

GUNDOGS such as the Cocker Spaniel (**5**) are trained to flush and retrieve game during a shoot.

OTHER WORKING DOGS are usually large and are used as guard, rescue or sled and cart dogs. The small French Bulldog (**6**) was used in bull-baiting.

TOY DOGS

CHIHUAHUA (1) 9 in.
From Mexico. The smallest breed in the world. Originally smooth-coated, a long-haired variety has also been bred.

TOY POODLE (2) 11 in.
The smallest variety of poodle. A popular pet for at least 500 years. Their long fluffy fur needs careful clipping and grooming.

SHIH TZU (3) 10½ in.
Affectionate dogs that were kept by Chinese Emperors and were known as "lion dogs." The Lhasa Apso is a similar dog from Tibet.

POMERANIAN (4) 11 in.
A miniature German Spitz with beautiful fur that needs daily grooming. Devoted to their owners but can be snappy.

PUG (5) 11 in.
Originally from China, these affectionate dogs were first brought to Europe by the Dutch.

BICHON FRISE (6) 12 in.
Friendly little dogs with a fluffy, curly coat. A pet of European aristocrats since the 1600s.

TERRIERS

JACK RUSSELL (7) 11–15½ in.
Named after the British
clergyman who first bred them
in the 1800s. Excellent rat-
catchers, these lively dogs are a
popular pet, but can be snappy.

YORKSHIRE TERRIER (8) 9 in.
Bred as a ratcatcher in the
Yorkshire coal mines, these
little dogs are now popular pets.
Their long, straight, silky hair
needs constant grooming or
should be cut to a shorter, more
manageable length.

WEST HIGHLAND TERRIER (9)
11 in. Originates from the west
coast of Scotland. It has a thick,
white coat that needs regular
grooming and clipping.

BRUSSELS GRIFFON (10) 8 in.
A small, flat-faced terrier from
Belgium. It can have a rough
coat (illustrated) or a smooth one.

HOUNDS

MINIATURE DACHSHUND (11)
9 in. Once used in Germany to
hunt badgers. Bred as smooth-,
long- and wire-haired varieties.

THE CAT

25 inches (nose to tip of tail)

Cats were sacred to the Egyptians, while other ancient people kept cats to protect their grain stores from mice. Today, most cats are still "free spirit" pets – we provide warm lodgings and food, the cat comes and goes as it pleases. Crossbred tabby (illustrated).

Train to use a litter box when needed. At 6–8 weeks, and annually, a kitten should be vaccinated against feline enteritis, flu, feline AIDS virus and rabies. Tattoo or microchip to identify the cat if lost. Apply sunblock to the ears of white cats to prevent skin cancer.

Cats are carnivores and must eat meat. There is a great variety of fresh, canned, moist and complete dried foods available. Do not overfeed, obesity leads to serious health problems. Will catch wild birds and mice, so treat for parasitic worms and fleas regularly.

Kittens must be spayed or neutered when 5–8 months old to avoid unwanted pregnancies – both in your own cat, your neighbors' and feral (stray) cats. Every year thousands of unwanted kittens are adopted or humanely destroyed by animal welfare agencies.

Cats can be loosely divided into a number of groups. Most people keep a **NON-PEDIGREE** or cross-bred cat. These familiar cats are either short-, semi-long- or long-haired and are tabby, black, white, ginger or tortoiseshell. Illustrated: a ginger shorthair (**1**).

PEDIGREE LONGHAIRED cats. The first longhaired cats came from Turkey and Persia during the 1800s. The most well known breed, the Persian, is bred in a wide range of solid colors such as Cream (**2**). Patterned Persians include tabby, tortoiseshell and colorpoint cats.

PEDIGREE SHORTHAIRED cats include solid (all one color) cats such as the Chartreux (**3**). Pedigree tabby cats are bred with perfectly matched markings. Other shorthaired cats include the Abbysinian (North Africa) and the Korat (Thailand). Rex cats have short, curly fur. Oriental cats include the popular Siamese – highly intelligent cats with long, sleek bodies, loud voices and strong personalities. The Oriental Shorthair (**4**) is a long-legged Siamese type, bred in a variety of solid colors and patterns such as tabby (illustrated).

CROSSBRED SHORTHAIR (1) The most common type of non-pedigree cat. Originally domesticated from tabby European Wild Cats, they now occur in a great variety of colors. Tortoiseshell cats are usually female.

CROSSBRED SEMI-LONGHAIR (2) Longhaired cats first came from the Middle East. Semi-longhairs do not have the flat, round faces of pedigree Persian cats.

CROSSBRED LONGHAIR (3) A non-pedigree Persian. The long fur needs to be groomed regularly to prevent matting. Apply flea treatments regularly.

PERSIAN (4) These gentle cats have wide, flat faces, pug noses and short legs. Their long, fine fur is often dense and thick, and requires at least 30 minutes grooming every day.

SIAMESE (5) Blue-eyed oriental cats with a short, creamy coat and points (darker markings) to the face, ears, feet and tail. Descended from sacred cats from Thailand, they first arrived in Europe in the late 1800s. Now bred in blue, chocolate, lilac and other color points. Loud, intelligent, sociable and demanding, these cats are usually devoted to their owners.

BURMESE (6) Descended from a single brown cat from the Far East that was taken to the USA in the 1930s. Intelligent, and friendly, Burmese are now also bred in blue, chocolate and lilac colors.

ABYSSINIAN (7) Often small cats that resemble the African Wild Cat. They may be descended from a cat that was imported from Ethiopia in Victorian times. They have short, ticked fur, ear tufts, dark tail tip and spinal crest. Varieties include Ruddy (illustrated), Red, Fawn and Blue. The Somali is an Abyssinian cat with long fur.

BIRMAN (8) A longhaired, cat from Burma. Has darker points to the face, ears, legs and tail, but the toes are white. Colors include tabby and tortoiseshell.

MAINE COON CAT (9) These come from the New England state of Maine. They are large, semi-longhaired cats whose waterproof coat needs little extra grooming.

CORNISH REX (10) Rex animals are those showing a genetic mutation that results in short, curly fur. Cornish Rex cats are descended from a single kitten, born to a farm cat in 1950.

CHINCHILLA RABBIT
14–18 inches, 5½–6½ lb

Domestic rabbits are descended from the European wild rabbit and have been bred since Roman times. Pretty Chinchilla rabbits make good pets; their gray and white coat looks like that of a Chinchilla from South America.

Provide a large, dry hutch at least 5 x 2 x 2 feet, which should be placed outside in a sheltered position, protected from the wind and shaded in hot weather. Line with newspaper and wood shavings, and provide timothy hay or straw for bedding.

Feed each day with 5 oz of dried rabbit mix and fresh foods such as fruit and fresh grass. Give unlimited fresh water and timothy hay. Rabbits need to gnaw to keep their teeth in good condition so give them apple wood, hard-baked bread and fibrous vegetables.

Domestic rabbits live for approximately 5–10 years. They breed prolifically, so keep bucks (males) and does (females) together only if you have the time, space and money to provide for their ever-growing family.

PATTERNED RABBITS

DUTCH, HIMALAYAN 4½–5 lb

These small, patterned rabbits are popular pets. The Dutch (**1**) rabbit has white front legs, saddle and blaze on its nose; the back, ears and cheeks are dark; often black, gray or chocolate. Himalayan (**2**) rabbits are white with dark ears, paws and nose.

Exercise rabbits in a wire run placed on clean grass that has not been treated with pesticides or fouled by other animals. Move the run regularly to provide more grass to nibble. Some rabbits can be trained to walk on a lead, but avoid passing dogs and cats.

Feed rabbits vegetables and fresh kitchen trimmings such as apple, carrot, various types of cabbage, celery, parsnip, turnip, raw potato (but not green) and spinach. Avoid giving too much lettuce (green leaf, not iceberg), tomato and cucumber.

Doe rabbits have up to 3 litters a year, with 2–8 babies (kittens) in each litter. Pregnancy lasts for 28–34 days. The doe makes a nest lined with her own fur, which she plucks out a day or two before giving birth. The kittens are usually born during the night.

NETHERLAND DWARF RABBIT

2 lb

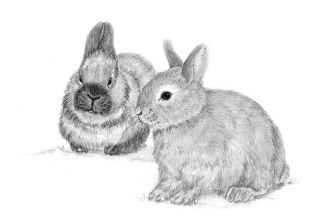

The smallest breed, Netherland Dwarfs are very pretty with short ears and cute rounded face. They are popular pets and come in virtually every color and fur pattern. Some rabbits are nervous, so choose a pet only from mild mannered parents.

Rabbits make ideal house pets. For safety, provide a cage for night time and when the rabbit is left alone. At all other times the house rabbit can be let out to explore – but protect electric cables with conduit to prevent chewing. It can be litter-trained like a cat.

Collect wild plants for your rabbit, such as freshly picked clean grass, dandelion, clover and plantains. Foraging for a variety of different foods helps a pet rabbit to stay mentally alert, but avoid roadside plants, which may be contaminated by gasoline fumes.

Newborn rabbit kittens are naked, blind and helpless. Keep the maternity cage covered with a cloth as soon as the mother starts to build her nest. Keep quiet when near the cage and do not touch the babies in the nest – the doe may kill them if they are disturbed.

1

2

Soft-coated rabbits with very long, floppy ears that hang down at the sides of the face. English (**1**) and French Lops are very large rabbits; they are intelligent and affectionate. Dwarf Lops (**2**) are smaller and make excellent pets.

When picking up a rabbit, start by placing a restraining hand on the shoulders or scruff of the neck; place the other hand under the chest behind the front legs; lift, and transfer the restraining hand under the back legs to support the rabbit's weight.

Do not give wilted or rotten green food to rabbits. Avoid giving too much lettuce as it can cause diarrhea. Cold vegetables taken straight from the refrigerator can cause stomach upsets. Avoid frosted greens during winter.

Baby rabbits grow fur when they are a week old. At 10 days their eyes open, and their ears at 12 days. After 18 days the kittens leave the nest and start to eat solid food but will suckle from their mother until 6–8 weeks old.

Rex rabbits are covered in a beautiful, dense, but short fur that looks like velvet. Only the soft under-fur is present, the long guard hairs seen in other breeds are absent. Bred in many colors including Fox (illustrated) and Sable. They make excellent pets.

Inspect your rabbit every day, in good light, to check that it is healthy. The fur should be clean and not matted, especially under the tail. Loose droppings indicate diarrhea or some other form of stomach upset.

Do not allow rabbits to eat poisonous plants such as the green parts of potato, many houseplants, garden shrubs and flowers. Learn to recognize the poisonous wild plants, such as Ragwort, Foxglove, Deadly Nightshade and Poppy.

Rabbits become sexually mature at 4–6 months. Separate the young bucks at 3 months or they will fight with each other and mate with their mother and sisters. Neutered bucks or two neutered does should be kept together for company.

Bred for their long, soft hair, the English Angoras (**1**) are big, round-bodied rabbits with fluffy ears. French Angoras (**2**) are larger and have normal, short-haired ears. The Jersey Woolly (**3**) is a small longhaired breed that is a popular pet.

Angora rabbits are often kept in a special wire-bottomed cage to prevent their wool from becoming matted and soiled. They must be carefully groomed with a wire brush and combed every day to keep the fur in good condition. The hair can be spun and knitted.

Pet rabbits often suffer from malnutrition that results in weak bones and deformed teeth. Like many animals they eat only the pieces of rabbit chow (which should contain no seeds) they like best. Make sure that the rabbit has eaten everything before refilling the bowl.

Kittens can leave their mother at 8 weeks old. When looking for a pet, choose an alert, inquisitive rabbit with bright eyes and twitchy nose. Look for a clean coat, clean eyes and ears, no diarrhea, quiet, even breathing and good teeth.

ENGLISH SPOT (1) 8 lb
White with dark spots. Dark color also on nose, ears, around eyes and in a line running down the back. Good pet.

HARLEQUIN (2) 8 lb
Golden-orange and black. Separate colors on either side of the head and in bands on the body. Good pet.

NEW ZEALAND (3) 11 lb
Large, usually white rabbit, bred for fur and meat. Can be aggressive. Not suitable for the inexperienced owner.

SABLE (4) 7 lb
Dark brown head, ears, legs and tail. Pale body. Good pet.

BELGIAN HARE (5) 12 lb
Large, lean rabbit with long legs and ears. Short red-brown coat. Hare-like. Not suitable for the inexperienced owner.

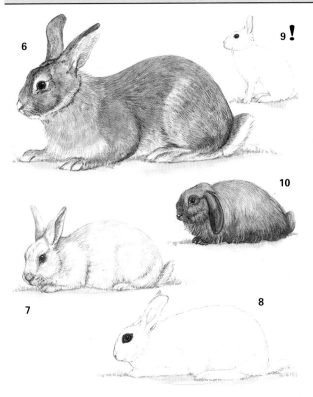

FLEMISH GIANT (6) 14 lb
Very large. The smallest weigh at least 11 lb. Good-natured. Needs a very big cage.

D'ARGENT (7) 8 lb
Dark under-fur overlaid with a paler shade gives the coat a silvery appearance. Also occurs in brown, blue, cream and champagne. Good pet.

BLANC DE HOTOT (8) 10 lb
A pretty, white rabbit with two black eyes. Also bred as a dwarf variety.

POLISH (9) 2¼ lb
A small, slim rabbit with short ears and long legs. Pretty, with attractive glossy fur, but can often be aggressive.

CASHMERE LOP (10) 5 lb
Small and fluffy, this breed is a longhaired Dwarf Lop. It is a popular pet but it requires regular grooming.

AGOUTI GUINEA PIGS

9–13½ inches, 1–1½ lb

SILVER

These shorthaired guinea pigs with ticked, wild-type fur, include Lemon, Cinnamon, Salmon and Golden varieties. The Silver Agouti (illustrated) resembles its wild ancestor, the South American Cavy, which was first bred for meat by native Americans before the Incas.

Keep a pair in an indoor cage, or a hutch, at least 36 x 18 x 24 inches, located outside, or in a shed. Protect from cold drafts; do not subject to extremes of temperature. Handle regularly to tame – but they will always play "catch the pig" to avoid being picked up.

Fresh water and a bowl of dried pellets for guinea pigs should be available at all times. Like humans, guinea pigs cannot produce vitamin C, so a variety of fresh hay, grass, vegetables, including watercress, and fruit must also be given daily.

Lifespan 4–8 years. Pregnancy 67–73 days. Babies are born "up and running" – fully furred, eyes open and able to take a few wobbly steps soon after birth. Boars (males) must be removed from the females after 6 weeks.

Shorthaired guinea pigs are bred in a great variety of solid colors:
Black, White, Albino, Red, Chocolate, Beige, Lilac, Cream (**1**),
Cinnamon, Golden. Satin guineas have a silky coat, while Rex
guineas are frizzy. Illustrated: Golden Satin (**2**), Chocolate Rex (**3**).

Clean the cage at least twice a week. Line with newspaper and/or
dust-free wood shavings. Use dry, mold-free hay – not straw, it
causes eye injuries – for bedding. The water bottle must have a
metal tube because guineas chew rather than lick when drinking.

Give at least a handful of fresh food a day. Give fresh kitchen
trimmings such as cabbage, carrot, beet, parsnip, turnip, celery,
beans, sweet corn, lettuce, spinach, zucchini, cucumber. Include
tops and roots where possible.

2–4 (sometimes 6) pups are born in each litter. Sows should have
their first litter when they are 5–10 months old. If a sow has her
first babies after she is 6 months old, the bones of her pelvis are no
longer flexible and she will have trouble giving birth.

The coat in these animals is patterned with solid blocks of color. Dutch (**1**) and Himalayan (**2**) guinea pigs resemble rabbit breeds, the Tortoiseshell (**3**), a cat. In Brindle, Roan and Dalmatian guinea pigs, the coat is speckled or has an even finer mix of colors.

During spring and summer, give guinea pigs exercise outside in a wire run placed on clean, untreated grass. Avoid wet and windy weather. Shade from direct sun and provide a water bottle; guinea pigs can suffer from heat exhaustion above 90°F.

Do not give a guinea pig too much spinach or lettuce. Carefully remove green or bruised portions from raw potato and peelings. Avoid thistles that may have been caught in a bale of hay – the sharp spines cause sore mouths.

Guinea pigs are social animals, and should be kept in pairs or in small groups, provided that there is enough cage space for each animal. Adult boars will usually fight, but two boars may live peacefully if they have been brought up together.

Rough-haired guinea pigs, each with a single rosette or whirl of fur on the top of the head. American Crested (**2**) guineas have a white patch of fur in the middle of the rosette, which the English Crested (**1**) lacks.

Grass is a guinea pig's natural and favorite food. Because hay is dried grass, it is not surprising that guinea pigs eat most of their bedding. Provide fresh timothy hay daily and clean the droppings corner. If possible, purchase hay in a bale and store in a dry place.

Guinea pigs enjoy fresh fruit. Give a few pieces of apple, pear, tomato, orange, grapes, melon, banana, peach, etc. Introduce new foods slowly – too much at once can cause upset stomachs. If a particular food is not liked, remove the next day to prevent rotting.

Guinea pig pups can leave their mother when weaned at 6–8 weeks. When choosing your pet look for: clean, healthy fur; dry around eyes, nose and mouth; quiet, even breathing, not wheezy; no diarrhea. Young guineas may appear to be timid and nervous.

These rough-haired guinea pigs have rosettes (whirls of fur) all over the body. Pure-bred Abyssinians always have the same number and position of whirls. All guinea pigs whistle and squeak at feeding time or purr when stroked, but this breed is particularly vocal.

Claws may need clipping from time to time; get a vet to show you how to do this the first time. Guineas may catch colds and respiratory diseases following temperature changes when they are moved from indoors to outside in winter, or if left in drafty or damp conditions.

Feed fresh, clean grass and, if possible other wild plants – but only if correctly identified. Collect bramble leaves (remove thorns), chickweed, plantain, vetch and clover. Avoid giving too many dandelions and groundsel, as they can cause diarrhea.

Remove the boar from the sow before pups are born. He will try to re-mate soon after their birth and may trample on the babies. Never keep rabbits and guinea pigs together. Even if they appear friendly, a rabbit can trample or kick its smaller guinea pig companion.

LONG-HAIRED GUINEA PIGS

PERUVIAN, SHELTIE, CORONET   9–13½ inches, 1–1½ lb

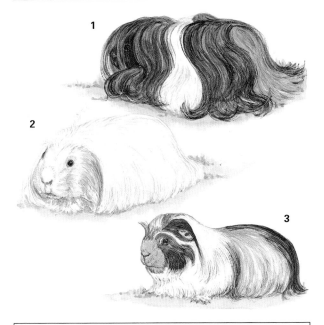

A Peruvian (**1**) guinea pig has long hair that grows towards and often over its head. It is sometimes difficult to tell which end is which! The hair grows back from the face in the Sheltie (**2**) and Coronet (**3**) – which also sports a single whirl on its head.

Longhaired guinea pigs need careful, regular grooming to remove dirt and tangles. Many owners cut the hair, because it can grow up to 18 inches in length. The hair of longhaired show guinea pigs is kept rolled up in paper or cloth "rollers."

Like other rodents, guinea pigs have a pair of chisel-like front teeth that grow continually. They need to gnaw apple wood, hard-baked bread crusts and other hard, tough foods such as melon skin, turnip, and corn stems to prevent overgrowth of the teeth.

An adult guinea pig may fight if an unfamiliar guinea is placed in its cage. Introduce two strangers in neutral territory, such as a box indoors. If they still fight, separate them with a wire screen or wash them in scented, mild shampoo, dry thoroughly and replace in box.

White mice have been known since ancient time and kept as pets and laboratory animals for the past 100 years. Mice are bred in hundreds of varieties of solid colors, such as Red (**1**), and patterns, such as Pied (**2**), similar to those seen in rabbits and other animals.

Keep a pair of mice in a narrow-barred, metal cage, at least 15 x 12 x 12 inches. Line with wood shavings, give shredded paper or tissues for bedding. Do not use cotton wool or other fibrous material – the threads can wrap around a mouse's legs and cause serious injury.

Mice eat a wide variety of foods. Mixed dried mouse food can be supplemented with pieces of hard, dried bread, good quality dog kibbles and breakfast cereals (not the sugary kind). Provide water in a small water bottle. Give fresh food three times a week.

Pet mice live for 2–3 years. They can breed after 6–8 weeks and pregnancy lasts for 21–28 days. 7–10 babies are born blind and naked. The babies and their nest should not be touched until their eyes open at 2 weeks.

Fancy mice are available in a number of coat varieties. In Longhaired mice (**1**), the coat is twice as long as in normal mice. Rex mice have bent whiskers and a slightly wavy coat. Satin (**2**) mice have beautiful glossy and shiny fur.

Plastic hamster tube systems provide a highly variable accomodation but check that tubes are fully cat-proof and escape-proof. Provide climbing platforms, ladders and treadmill wheels for exercise. Handle pet mice frequently to keep them tame.

Provide small amounts of fresh food such as fruit, and vegetables. Mice require a quantity of protein in their diet, so give them small amounts of cheese, milk, hard-boiled egg, lentils, beans and nuts (very fattening). Do not overfeed – too many tidbits make fat pets.

When choosing a pet mouse select one that looks bright and healthy, but is easy to catch and not overweight. Two female mice should be kept together for company if you do not want to breed from your pets.

STANDARD RAT
14–20 inches, 7–18 oz

ALBINO, BLUE

Affectionate, clean and intelligent, pet rats are descended from wild Norway (or Brown) Rats. Bred in laboratories since the early 1900s, Albino (**1**) and solid colors such as Blue (**2**) are now available. Silvered rats are solid-colored with overlying silver hairs.

Keep a pair of rats in a solid-floored cage that is at least 24 x 12 x 12 inches. Rabbit hutches, bird cages and aquarium tanks may also be used, provided they are suitably escape-proof. Fit a wire mesh top to a tank for safe ventilation.

Rats will eat virtually anything. Feed on commercial rat mix. For added variety you may also give small amounts of cereal grains, including rice, fruit and vegetables, meat and fish, hard-boiled egg, beans, etc.

On average, a pet rat lives for 2½ years. Rats are intelligent, socially interactive animals. In the wild they live in large colonies, so ideally, a same-sex pair (preferably litter mates) should be kept together for company.

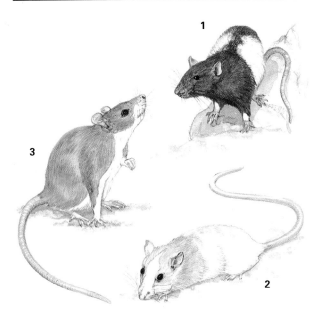

Hooded (**1**) rats are white with a dark- or pale-colored hood over the head and shoulders. Blaze (**2**) rats have a white blaze from nose to forehead. Berkshire (**3**) rats are colored with a white underside.

Line the cage or tank with wood shavings or peat, and provide shredded paper (not newspaper), tissue or hay for bedding. These affectionate animals love to be petted, and will ride in pockets or on their owner's shoulder.

Provide fresh food and water every day. Fruit, vegetables and meat deteriorate quickly in warm, moist conditions, so remove any stale food from the previous day. Like other rodents, rats need to gnaw on something hard to keep their teeth in good condition.

Rats become sexually mature at 6–8 weeks. Pregnancy lasts for 21–30 days. Place the pregnant female in a separate cage at least one week before the birth is due. At least 8–12 (sometimes 20) young are born in each litter.

Rex (**1**) rats have curly coats – either long and wavy, or short and curly. Satin rats have a shiny coat. Hairless (**2**) rats are bald; they were bred by crossing Rex with Rex, and then selecting those offspring to breed again that had the greatest loss of hair.

Hairless rats need to be kept warm. Choose an aquarium for this breed, with a tight fitting, wire mesh lid. It will be less drafty than an open-barred cage. Rats are very intelligent animals. Provide plenty of toys to exercise both mind and body.

Rats love to eat tidbits and leftovers; they will eat almost anything. It is very tempting to give a pet rat lots of tasty treats, but beware, because it can soon become grossly overweight. The same rules apply as for humans: reduce sugars, fats and the quantity of food.

The mother rat suckles her babies for about 3 weeks. Young rats can be purchased when they are 4–6 weeks old. Choose a frisky, healthy-looking rat with a smooth tail and sleek fur; check for clean ears, eyes and nose, and that there is no injury to feet or legs.

1

2

! see page 52

Popularly known as Golden Hamsters, these small rodents were first found in the Syrian desert. Most pet hamsters are descended from a single family that was collected in 1930. Today, Golden hamsters are bred in Light, Dark (**1**), and Normal (**2**) varieties.

Keep in a cage of heavy duty (chew-proof) plastic and galvanized metal, that is at least 16 x 12 x 12 inches. Line with a deep layer of peat and/or wood shavings. Provide shredded paper, tissues and hay for nesting material. Avoid fibrous bedding.

Wild hamsters eat a wide variety of plants, seeds and animal foods. Pet hamsters should be given dried hamster food, supplemented with pieces of vegetable, fruit, wild plants, cereals, nuts and hard-boiled egg.

Hamsters live for 1–3 years. They are solitary animals, so keep each adult hamster in a cage on its own. The young become sexually mature at 4–6 weeks old, after this time the adults will fight with each other unless they are separated.

49

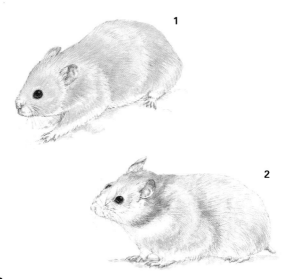

1

2

! see page 52

Syrian Hamsters have been kept as pets only since the 1940s. They are now popular throughout the world and breeders have produced at least 100 varieties. Solid-colored varieties include Cinnamon (**1**), Gray (**2**), and White.

Wild hamsters live in underground burrows – twisting tunnels with chambers used as bedrooms, storage areas and toilets. Hamster homes made of tubular plastic can recreate natural burrows and are great fun for pets and owners alike.

As well as hamster mix, small quantities of other cereals can add interest to the diet. Try pieces of hard bread, good quality dog kibble, barley, wheat, oats and chicken scratch or chicken feed. Corn and sunflower seeds (only small amounts) are favorite treats.

Hamsters are solitary animals, and adults will fight with each other. To breed hamsters place a male and a female in a box together. Watch carefully and separate them if they start to fight. After mating return the hamsters to their own cages.

PATTERNED SYRIAN HAMSTERS

TORTOISESHELL, BANDED, SPOTTED   6–8 inches, 3½–5½ oz

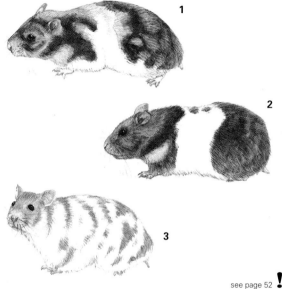

1

2

3

see page 52 ❗

Golden hamsters have been bred in a number of different fur patterns. The Tortoiseshell (**1**) is blotched with solid color, yellow and white. Banded (**2**) have a white band around the middle of their body. Spotted or Piebald (**3**) hamsters have white spots.

Hamsters are most active at dawn and dusk, especially from 8–11 pm. Provide an exercise wheel, fixed to the side of the cage (not one with open bars, which can cause leg injuries). If the wheel squeaks at night, lubricate with harmless cooking oil.

Give small pieces of fruit and vegetables such as carrots, salad, turnip, beans and peas, grapes and apple. Hamsters have a huge pouch in each cheek, which they tightly pack with food to carry back to their underground store.

Pregnancy in hamsters is very short and lasts only 15–18 days. Usually 4–12 pups are born, but some mothers may have more than 20 in a single litter. Cover the breeding cage and keep in a quiet place. Provide strips of paper for bedding.

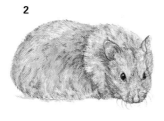

1

2

!

Angora (**1**) hamsters have long, soft hair. Generally pale in color, the hair is longest in male animals and forms a skirt at the side. Rex (**2**) hamsters have a short, soft wavy coat that feels like velvet. Satin golden hamsters have shiny, silky hair.

Angora hamsters must be brushed regularly – use a soft toothbrush. Hamsters become tame if handled, but they are nocturnal animals. Some can be grumpy and may bite if disturbed during their daytime sleep, so they may not be the best pet for young children.

Collect wild plants for your hamster from clean, untreated areas. Choose fresh grass, dandelion, plantain and clover. Hamsters also like nuts such as acorns, but never give them horse chestnuts - they are poisonous. Remember, nuts are fattening, so give only a few.

Baby hamsters are born at night and are nursed by their mother for 3–4 weeks. At birth the helpless pups are blind, deaf and naked. They can only crawl with their front legs. After 8 days the fur starts to grow and the eyes open at 12 days.

There are 25 species of wild hamster, some of which are also kept as pets. Chinese (**1**) and Russian (**2**) hamsters are small, gray, mouse-sized animals living in China, Northern Europe and Asia. Adults can be kept as single-sex pairs, either males or females.

Hamsters are active, inquisitive animals. Provide platforms and ladders to climb, and tubes and boxes to hide in. A branch of apple wood is good to chew and climb on. Clear, hollow balls are available to allow hamsters to run across the floor in relative safety.

Wild hamsters also eat animal food, such as earthworms. Give pets a few mealworms, scraps of lean meat or hard-boiled egg. Take care that small hamsters do not get large pieces of food stuck in their pouches, it can rot and cause serious health problems.

Hamster pups can leave their mother when they are 4 weeks old. Choose one that has bright eyes, is inquisitive and is happy to be picked up. The fur should be smooth, and the eyes, ears, nose and rear end should be clean.

MONGOLIAN GERBIL

7¾ inches, 1¾–2¼ oz

AGOUTI

Gerbils are small rodents that live in deserts and dry grasslands, from North Africa to China. There are many different species, but the Mongolian Gerbil is the most common pet. These intelligent, cheeky animals have been available only since the 1960s.

Keep gerbils in a large cage or tank, at least 24 x 18 x 12 inches. Cover the tank with escape-proof metal bars or mesh. Plastic and metal cages of the type sold for hamsters and mice are suitable. Line with a deep layer of peat or wood shavings – gerbils love to burrow.

Gerbils are desert animals. Their kidneys and other body organs actively conserve water, so these animals drink very little and pass very little urine. Nevertheless, fresh water in a small water bottle should always be available.

Wild gerbils live in small groups of a few males, females and their young. Keep pet gerbils in pairs or more, all of the same sex and preferably from the same litter. Adult gerbils that are not related may fight; try introducing new ones for a few minutes each day.

54

SOLID-COLORED GERBILS

ALBINO, LILAC, BLACK   7¾ inches, 1¾–2¼ oz

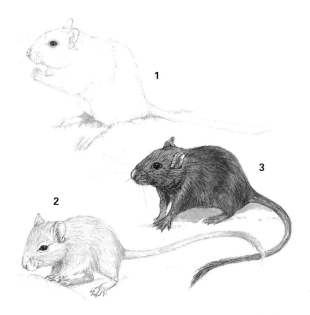

First kept as laboratory animals in the 1950s, gerbils have been captive-bred for a shorter time than most other pets and have produced fewer mutations and color forms. Albino (**1**), Lilac (**2**), Cinnamon and Gray are available. Black (**3**) appeared in 1978.

Gerbils like a nest box, big enough for all the family to sleep in together. Give shredded paper (not newspaper) or hay for bedding. Avoid fibrous, stringy bedding, which snags the gerbil's long legs. Provide platforms and ramps for climbing, and tubes to tunnel in.

Give a tablespoon of dried food per gerbil, per day. Use commercial gerbil food or a selection of the following: crushed oats, barley, wheat, corn or rye; sunflower seeds, pine nuts, peanuts; sugar-free breakfast cereal, good quality dog kibble, bread.

Male gerbils can stay with the female but should be removed before the young are born to prevent re-mating. Pregnancy lasts from 23–28 days. 5–7 pups are born, naked, deaf and blind. They grow hair within 6 days and their eyes open at 10–12 days.

PATTERNED GERBILS
7¾ inches, 1¾–2¼ oz *DARK-TAILED WHITE, CANADIAN WHITE SPOT*

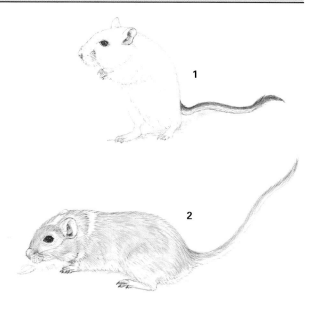

Most pet gerbils are Agouti or solid-colored. Patterned coats are not as common as in other pets. Dark-tailed White (**1**) is an albino with a darker tail. Canadian White Spot (**2**) has two patches of white fur, one on the top of the head, the other on the back of the neck.

Gerbils are intelligent, burrowing animals, so linked-tube hamster homes are ideal for this species also. Provide your gerbil with a variety of toys: wooden shapes, cardboard boxes and tubes, branches, fir cones, wooden cotton reels, rocks and logs to climb.

Small amounts of fresh food add variety to a gerbil's diet. Try pieces of green vegetables, green leaf lettuce, carrot, turnip, parsnip and fruit. Wild gerbils eat insects; give pets very small pieces of cheese, egg and meat.

Gerbil pups start to eat solid food after 16–20 days and are weaned by 21–24 days. They can remain with their parents until they are 8 weeks old, when males and females should be separated. Gerbils live for 3 years; females stop breeding when they are 2 years old.

Chipmunks have been kept as pets since the 1950s. While most species are North American, the most common pet is the Siberian Chipmunk from Northern Europe and Asia. Color mutations such as white and cinnamon occur in captive-bred animals.

These energetic animals dig underground burrows, but also climb trees. They need a very large, tall, aviary-like cage, with high nest-boxes, branches, shelves and ropes to climb. For burrowing, cover the wire floor with a deep layer of peat or bark and provide tubes.

Chipmunks store their food in hamster-like cheek pouches. Feed chipmunk mix containing peanuts, sunflower seeds, corn, oats, peas, etc. Give fresh vegetables, fruit (not peach stones), nuts in their shells, acorns and pine cones.

Live for at least 4-6 years. Keep as a pair of females, or 1 male and 1–3 females. Pregnancy lasts for 32 days. Do not disturb the mother after giving birth. Babies are born naked and blind but fur grows by day 16 and eyes open by day 28. Young leave the nest after 35 days.

CHINCHILLA
14 inches, 2 lb

STANDARD GRAY

These cuddly-looking rodents live high in the Andean Mountains of South America. They have some of the finest and thickest fur of all animals and have been bred on fur farms since the 1920s. Standard Gray chinchillas most resemble their wild cousins.

Keep in a heavy-duty, wire cage that is at least 36 x 24 x 24 inches. Line with a layer of wood shavings and hay that should be cleaned out every day to prevent the animal's fur becoming dirty and matted. Provide a brick to sit on, and a nest box to sleep in.

Chinchilla pellets, developed for fur farms, are a complete food. Buy in small quantities and check the sell-by date. Give 2 tablespoons of dried food each day and also fresh, dry timothy hay and fresh water. Wheat, barley, oatmeal, apple and millet can also be given.

Chinchillas live for 8–10 years, sometimes for as long as 20 years. Keep singly or as a breeding pair. Never keep 2 males or 2 females together, they will fight. Do not grab a chinchilla around the middle; if frightened their fur falls out or they may even lose their tail.

Selective breeding has produced a number of color mutations in chinchillas. These include White, Silver, Charcoal, Chocolate (**1**) and Beige (**2**). Silver and white animals may be patterned with small or larger blotches of gray or beige fur.

Provide each chinchilla with a dust bath – a deep metal tray containing fine bathing dust (obtained from a pet shop). Chinchillas love to dust bathe, they roll in it and play. This cleans grease and dirt from their fine fur that would otherwise become dirty and matted.

Chinchillas enjoy eating sunflower seeds. They are said to help make the fur shiny but avoid giving too many as they can result in an overweight chinchilla. Supplement dry food with small pieces of fresh fruit and green vegetables, as given to other rodents.

A doe chinchilla is pregnant for 111 days before giving birth to twins or triplets, born fully furred and with their eyes open. The buck can stay with the doe and pups but should be removed for a few days immediately after their birth to prevent re-mating.

FERRET
18–24 inches

1

Ferrets, first domesticated by the Ancient Egyptians, have been used to hunt rabbits and rats. Most of these small carnivores resemble their ancestor, the wild Western Polecat. Other colors have also been bred, including Albino (**1**), Cinnamon and Lilac.

Keep in a 2-story, wire cage, 30 x 18 x 18 inches. If wire-based, cover the floor with a washable carpet. Provide litter in a cat litter box, soft fabric to sleep on, toys to play with, including long tubes. Vaccinate against ferret distemper and rabies. Will walk on the lead.

Their wild relatives prey on small animals from rabbits to insects. Give pet ferrets commercial ferret food or kitten food. They also like small pieces of meat and cereal, cooked shrimp, cucumber, and fruit. Provide ample water and avoid overfeeding with tidbits.

Male ferrets are called hobs, the females are jills. They live for 8–10 years. Breeding is difficult, so most pets should be neutered hobs or spayed jills. Pregnancy lasts for 42 days; 6–12 kits in each litter. The kits do not open their eyes until 5–6 weeks old, just before weaning.

GREEN BUDGERIGARS
LIGHT GREEN, OLIVE 7 inches

1

2

Budgerigars, often popularly called parakeets, are tiny parrots that live in vast flocks in the Australian outback. Like wild birds, Light Green (**1**) budgies have a yellow head and green body; other varieties are the Dark Green and Olive (**2**).

Provide a cage that is long rather than tall, at least 30 x 18 x 18 inches. Line with paper and sprinkle with grit. Avoid sand sheets, which can cause sore feet and may be chewed. Give a bath every few days, in the sink or an enclosed bath that fits to the cage door.

Feed with commercially produced food – a mixture of various types of millet seed, canary seed, hemp and oats, with added vitamins and minerals. Provide fresh water at all times in a small water bottle or dispenser. Budgies love to peck millet sprays.

Budgerigars live for about 7 years. Birds that are kept singly are the best talkers but, as wild budgerigars are such social animals, pet birds should really be kept as a pair. They will preen each other for hours every day, chatter, play and feed together.

Blue budgerigars, with a brilliant body and white face, were first seen in 1910. They are bred in three shades of blue: Sky Blue (**1**) is the palest, Cobalt (**2**) is the brightest, middle shade, and Mauve (a deep blue with a purple tone), the darkest.

Budgerigars need natural perches of varying diameter, ½–1 inch. Narrow wood and plastic perches of uniform diameter can cause foot problems. Replace with thick and thin branches of fruit wood such as apple.

As they eat, budgerigars pick out each seed, crack it open and then drop the husk; as a result, their food soon becomes a mixture of whole seeds and empty husks. Every day, take the food container, hold over a garbage can, and blow gently to remove the husks.

Male and female budgerigars are distinguished by the color of the cere – the bald patch of skin at the base of the beak that surrounds the nostrils. This color difference develops after 6 months. In cock birds (male) the cere is blue, in hens (female) it is tan.

1

Gray budgerigars are actually a variant of the blue variety. They come in light, mid- and dark gray color forms. The White (**1**) budgerigar is an albino gray bird with red eyes, although the feathers may show a faint blue tinge.

Place the cage in a bright place that is not in direct sunlight or a draft. Budgerigars feel most secure if the cage is positioned high up (at about eye-level), against a wall, not in the middle of a room. Do not place in a kitchen, or in a room used by smokers.

Give a small amount of fresh green food and fruit every day. Try pieces of lettuce, spinach, wild plants such as dandelion, chickweed and groundsel, apple, carrot and orange. Grow millet in the yard from saved seed; feed fresh millet spray in late summer.

A nestbox will stimulate a pair to breed. Provide a nestbox that is 10¼ x 6¾ x 8 inches, with a 2-inch hole and a shallow depression in the floor. Budgerigars do not use any nesting material. The hen lays an egg per day for 5 or 6 days, and incubates them for 18 days.

Yellow budgerigars are recessive mutations of green birds in which the normal dark pigment is absent. There are no dark markings on the wings and head as there are in normal birds. Lutino budgerigars are similar, but have red eyes and pink feet.

Budgerigars should fly from their cage regularly. Birds that do not exercise become overweight and can suffer health problems such as heart attacks. Shut all doors and windows, close curtains and cover all glass and mirrors to prevent "flying into" accidents.

Budgerigars need iodine in their diet, so attach an iodine mineral block to the cage bars. A cuttlefish bone is a source of calcium and helps to keep the beak trimmed. Grit is not needed, it can block the gizzard. Seed bells and other toys help to prevent boredom.

The chicks are naked when first hatched; feathers start to grow after 8 days. They are fledged at 4 weeks and leave the nest one week later. While the hen is incubating the eggs, and for their first 2 weeks, she is fed by the cock – later he will feed the chicks as well.

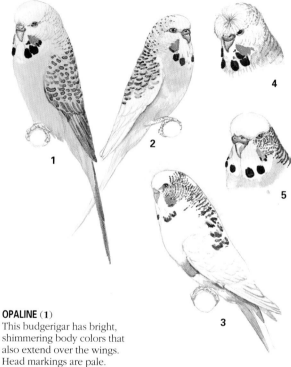

OPALINE (1)
This budgerigar has bright, shimmering body colors that also extend over the wings. Head markings are pale.

DOMINANT PIED (2)
A variety that has irregular patches of colored feathers on the body, which are either yellow (green birds) or white (blue birds).

HARLEQUIN (3)
Also known as Recessive Pied, this is a brightly colored bird with a great mix of colors.

CRESTED (4)
These budgerigars have a tuft of longer feathers growing on the top of the head.

YELLOW-FACED (5)
A blue bird with a yellow face rather than the normal white.

AFRICAN GRAY PARROT
13 inches

Central African parrots that have been pets since ancient times. Great mimics, and said to be the best talking parrots, they will copy words, sentences and even tone of voice. Growl at strangers, but devoted to their owners. Only hand-reared birds are really tame.

Can be kept in an aviary of heavy-duty wire (vertical bars only) on a metal frame. They do not like cold, damp weather, so heat in winter. Indoors, provide a tall cage, wide enough to spread the wings. Allow to fly regularly. Spray the plumage twice a week.

Feed parrot pellets supplemented periodically with sunflower seeds, peanuts, hemp, buckwheat, canary seed, pine nuts, flaked corn, and oats. Clean water, a cuttlefish bone and fresh fruit, roots and green vegetables should always be available.

They can live for more than 60 years and may have several owners throughout their lives. They will breed only if conditions are ideal. Nest in a large box, hollow log, or barrel. 3–5 eggs are incubated by the hen; the young hatch at 29 days and fledge at 11 weeks.

There are 24 species of Amazon parrot living in the rain forests of South America; 12 of them are rare or endangered. Only captive-bred birds should be purchased. The Orange-winged Amazon (**1**) and the Blue-fronted Amazon (**2**) are the most common pets.

Keep in a large aviary or indoor parrot cage. Allow extensive daily exercise and flight outside of the cage. Make perches in the room such as a forked branch held upright in a Christmas tree holder or a soil-filled flower pot. Place paper underneath to catch the mess.

All parrots should be fed suitable parrot pellets, plus fresh fruit and vegetables every day in separate containers. They also need fresh water. When bored or under stress parrots may pluck out their own feathers; an interesting, varied diet helps to avoid this.

Orange-winged Amazon parrots live for 40 years, Blue-fronted Amazons have survived for 90 years, so can easily outlive their owners. Good talkers but have a loud, harsh cry. Difficult to breed. 3–5 eggs are incubated for 26 days. Chicks fly after 8 weeks.

SENEGAL PARROT
10 inches

Small green parrots from the forests of West Africa. Hand-reared birds become very tame and make good pets. They whistle and speak a few words. Choose young birds with black eyes and pink base to the beak. By 12–18 months the eye becomes yellow.

May be housed in a garden aviary made of heavy duty vertical wires on a metal frame. Like other parrots they destroy anything made of wood. Provide shelter and heating in very cold weather. Indoors, keep in a large cage and allow free-flight regularly.

The basic food is parrot pellets. This can be supplemented with a seed mix. They first eat the pieces of mix that they like best. To keep them occupied with the rest give small amounts of food and add more only when the bowl is empty. Give fruit and greens daily.

Both male and female Senegal Parrots are very similar and difficult to tell apart. Breeding is difficult. The hen lays 2–3 eggs in a nestbox or hollow log. She will incubate them for 25 days. Destructive during the breeding season – provide extra branches to chew.

1

2

Magnificent Hyacinth Macaws (**1**) are the world's largest parrots. Wild birds live in the treetops of South American rain forests. Sadly, they are now rare due to over-collection and loss of their rain forest home. In the Scarlet Macaw (**2**), the sides of the head are bald.

Ideally, a pair should be housed in an aviary that is at least 20 x 6 x 6 feet. It should be constructed of steel and fitted with a lock that the birds cannot open – they are intelligent and particularly destructive. Provide a heated shelter and a large nestbox.

Use a pellet food but for interest supplement with peanuts, walnuts, hazelnuts, brazil nuts (in their shells), dried fruit, bread, chestnuts, fresh vegetables and fruit. Also give cooked white meat, bones, mussel and eggshells. A varied diet helps to alleviate boredom.

Rare Hyacinth Macaws should be kept only as breeding pairs. When they start to breed they will attack anybody close to the nest. 1–3 eggs are incubated by the female for 30 days. The chicks have feathers after 6 weeks but do not fly until they are 11 weeks old.

RING-NECKED PARAKEETS
16 inches
GREEN, BLUE

These small, long-tailed birds have the widest distribution of all parrots, ranging from Africa to China. Males have a dark collar around the neck. Normally Green (**1**), mutations have resulted in the Blue (**2**), Lutino (yellow) and Albino forms.

Keep in an aviary with a shelter, which should be used on cold nights or the birds will suffer from frost-bitten toes. Young birds can be kept in a large cage. Keep secure; some escapees now survive successfully in the wild.

Feed on a good quality parrot food. As with all dried food mixes, make sure that the package is fresh and within its expiration date. Out-of-date food may have deteriorated and will no longer contain a healthy selection of vitamins.

Place pieces of soft wood in the nestbox – the hen will break them up to form nesting material. 3–4 eggs are laid and incubated by the hen for 24 days. The cock feeds both hen and chicks, who will start to fly at 4 weeks. The collar develops when they are 2 years old.

Beautiful, vividly patterned parakeets from southeastern Australia. The Golden-mantled Rosella (**1**) has been bred for more than 100 years. Wild Crimson Rosellas (**2**) live in woodland and on farms; small flocks eagerly feed from bird tables. Musical whistle.

They are too active to be kept in a cage, so provide a garden aviary with at least a 12-foot flight, an insulated shed for winter roosting, and plenty of twigs and branches – they enjoy stripping the bark. Apple, pear and hawthorn are suitable types of wood.

Feed parakeet pellets and/or a commercial mix containing millet, hemp, canary seed, oats, pine nuts, buckwheat, sunflower seeds and peanuts. Give fresh fruit such as apple, and fresh greens. Also provide cuttlefish bones.

Keep breeding pairs alone, they are aggressive when breeding. Place a nestbox high up in a shady place. 4–8 eggs are incubated by the hen for 21 days. Young are nervous when they leave the nest at 6 weeks; they may fly into the aviary wire and be injured.

These small, crested parrots are widespread throughout the Australian outback. Popular as pets since the 1840s, they are the ideal parrot to choose for a novice owner. Varieties include Lutino (yellow), Albino, Pied, Cinnamon, White-faced, Pearl and Silver.

Suitable for a collection of several types of bird in an aviary; or keep in a large cage and allow free-flight exercise indoors. Keep two together for company. Obtained young, they quickly become tame. Males will sing tunes, say a few words or whistle melodiously.

Feed a balanced pellet food and, for interest, provide a mixture of sunflower and canary seed, millet, oats and hemp. Fresh water, cuttlefish bones and a mineral block should always be available. Provide a variety of fresh food such as fresh fruit and vegetables.

Cockatiels breed prolifically, especially in an aviary. 6–7 eggs are incubated by both the cock and the hen. The chicks start to hatch after 19 days, but the youngest often die. They leave the nest at 5 weeks, when their parents are preparing for the next brood.

Lovebirds are small parrots from Africa and Madagascar. There are 9 different species, from which many color mutations have been bred. Peach-faced (**1**), Masked (**2**) and Fischer's (**3**) are the most popular species kept as cage birds. These birds screech loudly.

Keep in a large birdcage or heated aviary with narrow-spaced bars. Lovebirds do not talk but will learn simple tricks. Provide swings, perches and other toys. All parrots, including budgies, are very intelligent and soon become bored without suitable entertainment.

Provide fresh water and pellets or Cockatiel seed mix at all times. Blow empty husks from the seed bowl every day and refill. Give fresh foods such as fruits, vegetables (including leaves), hard-boiled egg, rice and pasta.

Called lovebirds because they are so affectionate. Couples mate for life and must always be kept as a pair. Will build a nest from soft materials inside a wooden nestbox. 3–5 white eggs are incubated for 21–25 days; the chicks are fed by their parents for 5 weeks.

Like other cockatoos, the Lesser Sulfur-crested Cockatoo has a large crest of feathers, which is raised when the bird is excited or alarmed. Originally from the forests of Sulawesi and other Indonesian islands, these are popular cage birds.

Keep in a large, steel cage; provide plenty of out-of-cage exercise. Sociable and extremely intelligent, cockatoos demand a lot of time and attention from their owners; boredom will result in feather plucking, destructive behavior and loud, raucous screeching.

Feed a complete pellet mix or a good quality parrot mix containing sunflower seed, peanuts, hemp, canary seed and buckwheat. Give fresh food daily, including fruit and vegetables, such as apple, fresh coconut and spinach.

Cockatoos live for 40 years and will breed in an aviary. During breeding, the cock can be aggressive towards the female. 2–3 eggs are laid in a large nestbox. Both parents share the incubation for 28 days; the young leave the nest after 2 months.

CHATTERING LORY (1) 12 inches
A noisy, but colorful parrot from
Indonesia. They are good
mimics and talkers – they can
sound like a telephone ringing
and the person answering it.
Hand-reared birds can be very
tame. Lories are nectar-feeders,
and should be provided with a
sugary nectar solution in a
water bottle. Also give a wide
selection of fruit, vegetables,
greens and a small amount of
seed. They will breed in a
substantial nestbox. Provide
them with strips of softwood,
which they will shred for
nesting material.

SUN CONURE (2) 12 inches
This bird is a splendid mixture
of yellow, orange, red and
green. Conures are vivid parrots
from the rain forests of Central
and South America. They breed
well and make excellent pets if
selected from young, hand-
reared stock. Like lories,
conures are forest-dwelling
birds and should not be fed on a
diet of dried seeds alone. Give a
moderate quantity of small-sized
parrot mix and supplement with
a range of fruits, vegetables,
nuts, including brazils and
walnuts, rosehips and other
edible berries.

BORDER FANCY CANARY

5½ inches

Canaries are songbirds from the Canary Islands, taken to Europe by Portuguese and Spanish sailors in the 16th century. Border Canaries were bred in the Scottish borders. Plump and round-bodied, they come in many colors including variegated.

Keep in an aviary, or an indoor cage at least 24 x 18 x 12 inches. An all-wire cage or a box cage with solid sides and back are both suitable. Cover the floor with paper and sand and provide natural wood perches, fixed at least 4 inches from the sides of the cage.

Feed a good quality canary mix containing small seeds such as canary seed, hemp, rape, millet, linseed, poppy, and lettuce. Give fresh green food including spinach and parsley, apple and grated carrot. Provide a cuttlefish bone, grit and fresh water.

The breeding season lasts from April to May. Fix a cup-like nest pan, made of plastic, wood, basketware or wire, to the back of the cage and line it with a non-fibrous pad. Provide the birds with nest-building material such as dry moss, dried grass and soft hay.

GLOSTER FANCY CANARY

4½ inches

1

2

This is one of the smallest breeds, first developed in the 1920s in Gloucestershire, England. Some Glosters, called coronas, have a mop-like crest of feathers on their head (**1**). Other Gloster Canaries have plain heads – these birds are called consorts (**2**).

All cages should be square, not round, and as large as price and space permits. Place at eye-level against a wall. Wash and dry the cage bottom every week. Clean the bars and perches. Put your birds in a smaller, temporary cage until their home is clean and dry.

Wild finches eat insects, grubs and green food throughout spring, summer and autumn. Seeds are eaten only during winter. Give canaries softfood – a paste of bread and biscuit crumbs, ground rice, mashed hard-boiled egg and honey.

The hen lays 3–4 eggs and incubates them for 14 days. Provide soft food for breeding birds to feed to the chicks. Gloster corona birds carry a lethal gene, so coronas should not be cross-bred or the chicks will die. Always breed a corona with a consort.

Breeders are always seeking to produce young birds with progressively brighter plumage. Red Factor Canaries were produced by crossing a female yellow canary with a male Red Siskin from South America. Cross-breeding has since produced bright red birds.

Like other birds, such as budgies, canaries enjoy having a bath every day. A birdbath that hangs over the open door of a cage is easy to use. Many have a plastic cover that reduces splashes. Some free-flying birds bathe in the sink or even a shower.

The color of these birds varies, depending on the food that they eat before and during the molting period in July. Carrot, oats and niger seed enhance the red color. Egg yolk, rape seed and spinach improve yellow plumage, so avoid giving to red birds.

The chicks are fledged after 2 weeks and are ready to leave their parents a week later. The hen lays another clutch of eggs almost immediately, often while the chicks are still in the nest. Provide a second nest – the cock will continue to feed the first chicks.

NORWICH (1) 6¼ inches
These canaries have been bred
since the 1850s. They are bred
for their shape – a large, but
stocky body. Available in many
colors, including variegated.

LIZARD (2) 4¾ inches
The only surviving patterned
variety of canary. The body is
covered with rows of blotched
feathers called spangles.

FRILLED (3) 6¾ inches
These canaries are covered in
curly feathers that stick out in all
directions. First bred in Holland
in the 1700s, there are many
varieties, often named after
cities. Available in all colors.

ROLLER (4) 4¾ inches
These canaries have been bred
for their song for 200 years – the
males are the opera singers of
the canary world. Originally
from Germany, their song was
said to mimic the sound of the
mountain streams nearby.

SCOTCH (5) 6¾ inches
This variety is trained to stand in
a peculiar, hunch-backed stance
when exhibited at canary
shows. Belgian canaries are a
similar variety.

ZEBRA FINCH
4½ inches

1

Zebra Finches live in open countryside throughout Australia – they were first taken to Europe in the mid 1800s. Male birds have orange cheeks, females are less brightly colored. More than 40 color varieties occur, including White (**1**), Fawn and Pied.

Can be kept with other species in a winter-heated aviary, or indoors in an all-wire cage or box cage with a wire front. A cage, 30 x 20 x 18 inches or larger, is suitable for a pair of these sociable birds. Provide fruit-wood perches. They have a pleasant cheeping call.

Wild birds eat grass seeds, insects and plant food. Give canary seed and millet, softfood including chopped egg and mealworms, and greenfood such as lettuce, spinach, cabbage, fruit, chickweed, dandelion and the green seed heads of fresh grasses.

Zebra Finches live for 5 years. Easy to breed, they perform a courtship dance before mating. Provide a nest basket and nesting material. 4–6 eggs are incubated for 12–14 days. Give softfood for the parents to feed their chicks, which fledge after 18 days.

BENGALESE FINCH

4 inches

These are domesticated birds that are not found in the wild. They were bred in either China or Japan more than 200 years ago by crossing two or more species of Asiatic Mannikin finch. Several varieties, including Fawn, White, Chocolate and Chestnut.

Can be kept in an unheated aviary in a mixed flock. Bengalese Finches are very easily cared for and make an ideal first finch. Keep a pair in a box cage, 30 x 20 x 18 inches, lined with paper and bird sand. Replace perches with natural, fruit tree branches.

Feed a finch mix of canary and millet seeds, and a selection of vegetables and fruit. Soft food, chopped egg and mealworms will be a suitable substitute for the insect portion of a wild finch's diet. Also give grit, cuttlefish bone and fresh water.

They live for 5–8 years. Breed prolifically and are often used as foster parents. Build an untidy nest in a nestbox. The cock sings to the hen and fans his tail. 4–8 eggs are incubated by both parents; the eggs hatch in 14 days and the chicks fledge at 21 days.

RED-CHEEKED CORDON BLEU
5 inches

One of three similar species from Central Africa, they are actually a type of waxbill. The cock has bright red cheek patches; the hen is generally paler in color. Buy captive-bred birds, as imported birds take a long time to acclimatize to northern weather conditions.

Keep indoors in a large cage, or acclimatize to live outside in an aviary. These birds do not like the cold or damp, so provide a well-lit, heated shelter in winter. Plant the aviary with shrubs and bushes; provide natural wood perches in both aviary and cages.

Feed a foreign finch mix of millet and plain canary seed. Also give fresh grass seed heads, soaked seed and fresh millet sprays. Nectar (sugar water) can be given in a drinker or soaked into plain sponge cake. Small insects, grit and cuttlefish bones should also be given.

They live for 8–15 years. During courtship the male displays with a piece of grass in his mouth. The nest is dome-shaped, in a bush, nestbox or basket. 5 eggs are incubated by both parents for 14 days and the chicks fledge in 3 weeks. Must be fed live insect food.

Also known as the Indian Zosterops, these warbler-like birds are found from India to China. They are named for the distinctive white ring around each eye. There is little difference between the sexes but only the cock has an attractive, melodious song.

They prefer a large aviary that is well-planted with vegetation but suffer from the cold, so provide a heated shelter or bring indoors in cold weather. White-eyes take frequent baths to keep their plumage in good condition – provide a bath or spray with warm water daily.

Feed on diced fruit and softbill pellets or food. Give nectar in a feeder or soaked in cake; also insects such as small mealworms, fruit-flies, aphids, spiders, crickets. Give various fruits including apples, pears, bananas, oranges, grapes, grated carrot, berries.

They live for 10 years. The nest is built in a bush or an open nestbox. 3–4 eggs are incubated for 14 days. The parents must be given live insect food to feed the chicks, which leave the nest in 14 days. Breeding pairs are aggressive and will even attack their own fledged young.

A small thrush-like babbler that ranges from the Himalayas to southern China, including Assam and Burma. The male has such an attractive, flute-like song that he is also called a Pekin Nightingale. Active and inquisitive, these birds are easily tamed.

Keep in a well-planted aviary, with an insulated shelter for winter use (may need heating in cold weather). Pekin Robins bathe several times a day; a plant-pot saucer, filled with water and set into the ground, makes a cheap but effective birdbath. Replace water daily.

Eat a wide variety of foods including fruits, softbill food, millet and canary seed, soaked millet sprays, green foods such as vegetables and peas, live insects. If kept with other birds, they may steal their eggs and chicks. Can be tamed to eat mealworms from the hand.

They live for 10 years. A cup-shaped nest of twigs, grass and moss is built in a bush or a nestbox or basket, especially if it is placed behind a shrub or potted trees. 3–4 eggs are incubated for 14 days; chicks leave the nest after 2 weeks. Feed parents live insect food.

GREATER HILL MYNAH

Mynahs live in Southern Asia, from India to Indonesia and were kept by the ancient Greeks, who considered that they were sacred. They can mimic speech with remarkable clarity. There are several varieties, differing in size and the shape of the fleshy yellow wattle.

Suitable for a large, dry aviary or a long box cage, at least 40 x 20 x 20 inches, indoors. Provide plenty of free-flight exercise and bathing. Clean the cage often – Mynahs are messy eaters. They need plenty of mental stimulation (moving toys, mirrors) or become bored.

Feed a mixture of fresh fruit, with softbill food or Mynah pellets. Give insects such as mealworms, grasshoppers, fruit flies and aphids. Will also eat cottage cheese and minced beef. Give cubes of fruit such as cherry, berries, melon, apple, grape, gooseberry.

They live for 8–10 years. Will nest in a large nestbox or hollow log. 2–3 eggs are incubated for 14 days, and the young fledge after 20 days. Give live insect food to the parents. Some young, called gapers, may need to be hand-reared if attacked by their father.

RACING PIGEON
13 inches

Domestic pigeons, descended from wild Rock Doves, were kept by the ancient Egyptians, Persians and Greeks – either as sacred birds, for their ability to fly home and carry a message, or for meat. Today there are many hundreds of fancy breeds.

Keep free-flying birds in an aviary or pigeon loft – any ventilated structure from a garden shed upwards. Fit a landing platform and a trap-door permitting access in but not out. Inside, provide inverted V-shaped perches, open nestboxes and a large bathing tray.

Pigeons are grain feeders, so give a mixture of corn, wheat, rye, barley, oats, dried lentils, peas, beans, and smaller seeds including millet, sunflower, hemp, rape, linseed and canary seed. Water, grit and greenfoods should also be available.

Provide a nest-bowl, preferably of stoneware. Pigeons make a loose nest of straw and sticks. 2 eggs are incubated for 17 days. The chicks (squabs) are fed "crop milk," a liquid secreted by both parents. At 24 days the squabs are ready to start race training.

Pure white doves, with extra tail feathers that can be splayed out like a fan. These birds probably originated in India. They are one of the oldest breeds and were described in 1150 in Spain. They may be blue, brown or gray if a parent mated with feral city pigeons.

Pigeons were bred for food in medieval Europe and doves were kept in every village. Some of the old dovecotes in which they lived are still in use today. Keep in a large aviary with free-flying access, or in a modern pigeon coop attached to a building or on a tall pole.

Feed as for racing pigeons but reduce the quantity of peas, beans and lentils. Fantails are not quite as athletic as racing pigeons. Free-ranging birds will also forage for their own food around the farmyard or garden.

As in other domestic pigeons, the cock will pursue the hen and display by throwing back his head, puffing up his chest and fanning the tail feathers. The couple will also "bill and coo". Squabs are independent at 4 weeks, when the adults will nest again.

DIAMOND DOVE

8 inches

A tiny, long-tailed dove that lives near water throughout the Australian outback. It has a distinctive red ring around the eye. The white spots on the back and wings are larger in the male. Several varieties have been bred, including Silver, Fawn, Blue, Red, Yellow.

House them indoors in a large cage or in an aviary outside, as long as a warm winter shelter is provided. They are tolerant of other birds, so may be kept with a collection of mixed finches. However, they will attack other doves, so keep together only as a breeding pair.

Forage on the ground like other pigeons and doves. Feed a mixture of small seeds, including canary seed, millet, hemp and rape. They should also be given a variety of greenfoods, softfood and soaked millet. Grit, cuttlefish and fresh water should always be available.

They build a loose nest of twigs, hay and grass in an open-fronted nestbox or a canary nesting pan. 2 eggs are incubated for 13 days by both birds. Squabs leave the nest after 14 days; isolate them from their parents as soon as they are weaned to prevent attacks.

Small freshwater fish from South America, Trinidad and Barbados, but also introduced into other tropical areas to control mosquitoes by eating their larvae. Captive-bred Guppies come in a variety of colors and tail-types, including Veiltail (**1**), Delta (**2**) and Sword.

Suitable for a mixed collection of fish in a tank that is at least 24 x 15 x 12 inches. Choose a tank with the biggest surface area possible, allowing 12 square inches of surface area for each inch of fish length in the collection. Maintain water temperature at 72–82°F.

Guppies eat small crustaceans, worms and insects such as mosquito larvae. They will also take a quantity of plant matter and fine grade dried tropical fish food. They thrive on brine shrimp, daphnia and tubifex worms given live, or as freeze-dried blocks.

Guppies are prolific livebearers – females produce young every 4 weeks. Keep breeding males and females in a small tank. Females become swollen with young (fry) that are born live and swimming. Isolate adults in a wire cage to prevent them from eating the fry.

CARDINAL TETRA
1¾ inches

These popular aquarium fish originate from the warm waters of the Orinoco and Rio Negro rivers in South America. They are well known for their red flanks and vividly iridescent, electric blue body stripe. The water temperature should range between 73 and 79°F.

Suitable for a small tank (18 x 12 x 12 inches), but ideally kept in a large tank, as a small shoal in a mixed community of other species. Cover the base of the tank with well washed gravel, provide rocks and bark refuges, and plant with a variety of warm-water plants.

Eat worms, crustaceans and insects, plant material and fine-grade dried tropical fish food. Live brine shrimps can be hatched from pots of dry eggs that remain dormant until covered with salty water. Feed young shrimp to small fry, and adult shrimp to bigger fish.

Will breed in slightly acidic water, in a tank planted with bushy plants. Spawning takes place after the male drives the female into the plants. The eggs are scattered and stick to the plant leaves. The tiny fry are difficult to feed; give infusoria (microscopic food).

A member of the group of fishes known as cichlids, Angelfish have deep flattened bodies and long trailing fins. This body shape, striped in black and silver, helps to conceal Angelfish in their natural habitat – the reed beds of the Amazon and its tributaries.

Keep in a large tank, at least 24 inches long, furnished with rocks and planted with tall, narrow-leaved plants such as *Sagittaria* and *Vallisneria*. Angelfish are mid-water swimmers. They may be kept with a community of other fish of similar size. Maintain at 72–86°F.

Feed on flaked, dried tropical fish food and cubes of freeze-dried live food, stuck to the aquarium glass. Do not overfeed tropical fish. Uneaten food, especially if it has been commercially produced, rapidly decomposes and fouls the water – remove by siphoning.

Angelfish lay their eggs on vertical surfaces such as rocks, a piece of slate placed vertically, plant stalks and leaves. The parents guard their brood until the eggs have hatched and the fry are able to swim and look after themselves.

OTHER TROPICAL FISH

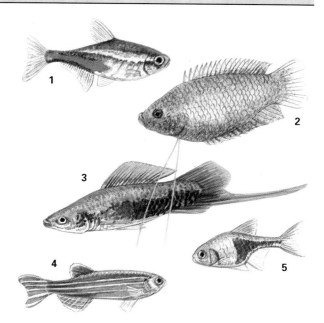

NEON TETRA (**1**) 1½ inches
From the upper Amazon. Similar
to the Cardinal Tetra, but the
bright red flank patches cover
only the tail. Water: 70–79°F.

HONEY GOURAMI (**2**) 1¾ inches
From N. India and Bangladesh.
Ventral fins are reduced to
feelers to probe for food. The
eggs are laid in a floating
bubble nest. Water: 75–79°F.

SWORDTAIL (**3**) 4¾ inches
From Mexico and Guatemala.
Males have a long, sword-like
tail and actively display to their
rivals. A surface feeder suitable
for a mixed species tank. Various
color forms. Water: 70–79°F.

ZEBRA DANIO (**4**) 2 inches
From Eastern India and
Bangladesh. Active swimmers
and surface feeders. Keep as a
shoal in a mixed community
tank. Easily bred, but place a
net between the adults and the
base of a breeding tank or the
parents will eat their own eggs
as they fall to the bottom.
Water: 65–77°F.

HARLEQUIN FISH (**5**) 1¾ inches
Active fish from Thailand and
Malaysia. They are well suited to
life in a community tank.
Provide plenty of water plants –
eggs are laid on the underside of
broad leaves. Water: 72–77°F.

OTHER TROPICAL FISH

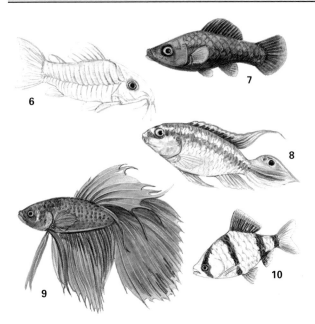

BRONZE CORYDORAS (**6**) 2¾ in. From South America and Trinidad. A small catfish with 3 pairs of barbels surrounding the mouth – they probe the gravel in search of food. Keep 2–6 individuals in a mixed tank. Water: 66–79°F.

BLACK MOLLY (**7**) 2¾ inches A hybrid of the Pointed-mouth Molly from Central America. A popular fish in mixed species collections available in a variety of color forms. Water: 73–82°F.

DWARF CICHLID (Kribensis) (**8**) 4 in. Known as "Kribs," these cichlids come from W. Africa. Keep a pair in a mixed tank. Will spawn inside a flower pot or other hideaway. Water: 75–82°F.

SIAMESE FIGHTING FISH (**9**) 2½ in. From S.E.Asia. Only the male has long fins and tail. Male fish are particularly aggressive to one another and will fight. Keep a single male with 1 or 2 females. The eggs are laid in a bubble nest, produced and guarded by the male. Water: 77–82°F.

TIGER BARB (**10**) 2½ inches From Borneo and Sumatra. A small shoal of these active, mid-water fish can be kept in a mixed tank. May attack other fish if the tank is too overcrowded. Water: 68–77°F.

Tropical coral reef animals and plants can be maintained in a home aquarium. Common Clownfish (**1**) and the Pajama Cardinal (**2**), from the Indo-Pacific Oceans can be kept with other reef animals, such as anemones, hermit crabs, corals, shrimp and starfish.

Fill a well lit aquarium, at least 36 x 15 x 12 inches, with synthetic seawater heated to a constant 75–79°F. Water must be tested regularly for pH (8.0–8.3) and ammonia (0) levels. Fit an aerator and filters, add sand and a rocky substrate for anemones and corals.

Feed fish live or frozen brine shrimp, morsels of fish meat, shellfish, squid, lobster eggs. Dried, flaked fish food is available for marine fish but is often rejected by Cardinals. Anemones, crabs, shrimp and starfish will eat pieces of fish and shellfish.

Clownfish are born male, but dominant fish change sex to become females. A pair adopt an anemone and spawn on rocks protected by its tentacles. The fish clean the spawning site and lay the sticky eggs onto the rock. The eggs are guarded by the male for 10 days.

COMMON GOLDFISH

1½–18 inches

First bred in China over 1,000 years ago, Goldfish are coldwater fish descended from a golden variety of wild Crucian Carp. Successive breeding from common goldfish stock has led to a great variety of color, body and fin shape.

Goldfish can live all year in an outside pond, or in a tank, 36 x 15 x 12 inches. Line with washed gravel, place rocks for cover and plant with oxygenating plants. Scrape green algae from the glass regularly. A filter will keep the water clean and improve aeration.

Goldfish flakes and granules are available from pet shops. Live or frozen food such as water fleas and tubifex worms, rolled oats, chopped earthworms, maggots, and lettuce can also be given. Do not overfeed or the water will become cloudy and the fish will die.

Goldfish may live for 25 years. They will breed in ideal conditions – good food, clean water, a garden pond or large tank, and water temperatures of 60–70°F. The female releases up to 5,000 eggs as the male chases her to fertilize them. Baby Goldfish are brown.

FANCY-TAILED GOLDFISH
8 inches

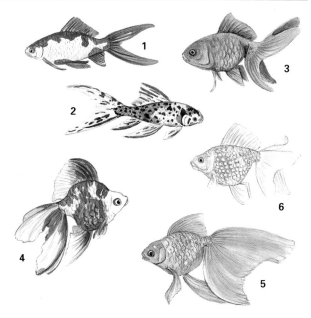

COMET (1)
A fast swimming goldfish with a long single tail. Bred in a variety of colors that include red and white. May be kept in a garden pond throughout the year. Can live to 14 years.

SHUBUNKIN (2)
Long-bodied and single-tailed like a Common Goldfish, but brightly colored in blue, red, yellow, brown, violet, with black spots on body and tail.

FANTAIL (3)
Short, egg-shaped body and twin tails held stiffly behind. Comes in metallic or calico color varieties.

RYUKIN (4)
Very short, spherical body that is often hunch-backed so that the double tail is held down at an angle.

VEILTAIL (5)
Short egg-shaped body with a tall dorsal fin, and very long and wide twin tails that hang down in beautiful folds. Keep in an aquarium.

PEARLSCALE (6)
A Fantail with thick, domed and white body scales that look like rows of pearls.

ORANDA (1)
Short, egg-shaped body with twin tails and dorsal fin. Large, berry-like growth on the top of the head. Keep with other slow-moving fish.

LIONHEAD (2)
A short-bodied fish with no dorsal fin and short tail fins. A berry-like growth covers the head and face. Aerate the water as gill activity may be impaired.

POMPON (3)
Goldfish with soft, fluffy growths, called pompons, above the nose. The pompons may be sucked into the mouth every time the fish breathes.

MOOR (4)
A jet black veiltail with protruding, telescopic eyes. There may be some gold coloration to the flanks, nose and belly.

CELESTIAL (5)
Weak swimmers with no dorsal fin. The eyes in these fish face upwards towards the sky – hence their name. Each eye is surrounded by a fluid-filled sac. Feed surface floating foods.

BUBBLE-EYE (6)
Similar to the Celestial, but each eye is surrounded by a huge, balloon-like sac that wobbles and moves as the fish swims.

97

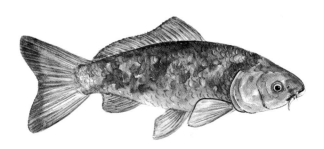

Wild carp were first domesticated by the Chinese and Japanese in ancient times. Brightly colored, Koi Carp were bred by Japanese farmers in the 17th century. Ghost Koi are fish that have interbred freely and are now reverting back to the ancestral domestic type.

Keep Koi in a large pond lined with butyl sheet, concrete or pre-formed fiberglass. The pond should range in depth from planted shallow margins of 20 inches, to a 4-foot deep central refuge. If possible fit a filter, and a fountain or waterfall to aerate the water.

Koi eat both plant and animal food. Supplement dried flakes and pellets with pieces of shredded lettuce, fresh shrimp, fish, earthworms, water shrimps, daphnia and tubifex worms. Tadpoles are also a favorite meal, so protect any that hatch in your pond.

Koi can live for 40 years. The spawning season lasts from spring to autumn. Females release many thousands of sticky eggs that become attached to water plants. Remove egg-covered plants to a breeding tank to prevent parents eating the eggs and fry.

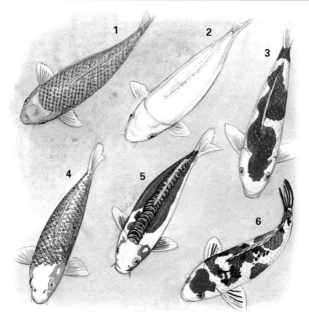

Koi are always patterned in one or more of the following colors: white, black, blue, red, orange, yellow, brown, silver or gold. They also come in a variety of scale types: *normal* (**3**,**6**), *metallic* (**1**), or *matsuba* (**4**) – scales with colored edges that give a pine-cone effect. The body scaling in *doitsu* fish is reduced to three lines of large mirror scales (**5**) or is virtually absent in *leather* fish (**2**).

Popular one-colored fish include the metallic gold **OGON** (**1**), and the **SHIRO OGON** (**2**), a platinum-colored fish. Pure white fish called Shiro-muji are eagerly collected in Europe and the USA but are regarded as worthless in Japan.

KOHAKU (**3**), the most popular two-colored fish, are white with a red pattern over the head and body. The red and blue **ASAGI** (**4**) is one of the oldest two-color breeds. **SHUSUI** (**5**) is a mirror-scaled variety of Asagi.

TAISHO-SANKE (**6**) are three-colored fish, with red patterns on white and black markings.

Crossbreeding has given rise to four-colored fish and the Goshiki which is a Koi with five colors.

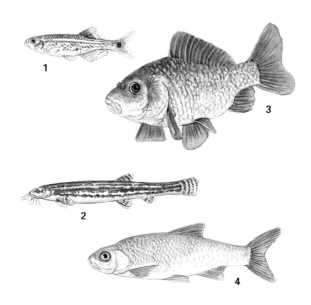

WHITE CLOUD MOUNTAIN MINNOW (1) 2¾ inches

Small, lively minnows from the White Cloud Mountain gorges in Canton, China. Keep a small shoal of at least four fish in a well planted, unheated aquarium. Feed flaked food, daphnia and brine shrimp.

WEATHER LOACH (2) 5½ inches

A small eel-like fish from Eastern Europe. Normally brown with dark spots and speckles, Golden Loach can also be obtained. A bottom-dweller, it has 10 barbels around the mouth to locate food in the sediment. Feed flaked food and daphnia.

CRUCIAN CARP (3) 10–20 inches

A deep-bodied relative of the Goldfish with bronze-colored scales and rounded fins. Wild Crucian Carp live in ponds, canals and rivers throughout Europe. Feed goldfish food, worms, daphnia and soft plant material.

GOLDEN ORFE (4) 24 inches

A slim, fast-swimming fish from N. European lakes and rivers. Keep a small shoal of these surface-dwellers in a large pond; they may jump out of smaller ponds. They will eat pond fish food, flakes, insect larvae, worms and snails.

HERMANN'S TORTOISE

12 inches

From southern Europe. These used to be the most popular pet tortoises. Millions were collected for pet shops – but most died. They are now an endangered species, available only as captive-bred animals. Protected in the Massif des Maures, southern France.

Active in temperatures 68–95°F and will hibernate during cold winter months. Adults need at least 20 square feet walking space; a large pen in the yard, or greenhouse in cooler weather, is ideal. Provide shade from the sun and a weather-proof sleeping box.

Provide a variety of food plants including lettuce, cabbage, dandelions, tomatoes, carrots, fruit and melon. Bean sprouts are particularly nutritious before and after hibernation. Will also eat earthworms. Give multivitamin drops. Can live up to 100 years.

Hibernate from November to March in a straw-lined box placed in a cool cupboard or frost-free garage. Young tortoises and weak, underweight adults should be kept active in a heated, well lit terrarium. If eggs are laid, incubate in a warm closet.

OTHER TORTOISES

SPUR-THIGHED TORTOISE (1) 12 in. Similar to Hermann's but has a short, horny spur on each thigh. Eats fruit, vegetables and salad, with occasional cat food and egg. Wild tortoises live in dry scrub from Morocco to Spain. Especially active between 77 and 95°F. Hibernates in winter.

RED-FOOTED TORTOISE (2) 20 in. Live in Central and South America. They have red scales on the head and legs, and orange spots on the shell. Can graze on grass in warm weather. Feed on fruit, vegetables and salad. Adults (not young) can occasionally be given a little cat food.

ASIAN STAR TORTOISE (3) 11 in. An attractive tortoise from India and Sri Lanka. The high-domed shell is patterned with yellow, star-like markings against a dark background. Can live outside in warm weather, or indoors in a terrarium maintained at 80–86°F. Feed as for other tortoises.

BOX TORTOISE (4) 8 in. A type of turtle from the eastern USA. The shell is hinged and can close up when the animal withdraws. Prefers humid, cool conditions (64–82°F). May not need to hibernate in warmer climates. Feed on fruit and vegetables, insects and worms.

!

Also called the Red-eared (Pond) Slider, this terrapin from the southeastern United States has a bright red band behind each eye. Wild sliders live in rivers, ponds and swamps and are often seen basking on top of each other on a favorite sunny log.

Keep a pair of adults in a large but shallow tank, at least 48 x 18 x 24 inches. Half-fill with water and fit a submersible filter or it will get very dirty. Make a dry island from rocks or cover a shelf with gravel. Heat with a spotlight for basking but provide a bark refuge.

Feed young turtles once a day on small crustaceans, maggots and mosquito larvae, earthworms and snails. Dried or frozen turtle food is available. Adult turtles should be fed once every 2–3 days; include fresh meat and plant food such as lettuce in their diet.

Eggs (2–23) laid during June and July, eventually hatch 8–10 months later. Baby turtles grow quickly and reach maturity in 2–5 years. Adults can bite and are not suitable for young children. All turtles carry salmonella, so always wash your hands after handling.

PAINTED TURTLE
10 inches

! see page 103

Widespread throughout the USA, except in the southwest and Florida. They live in slow-moving rivers, weedy ponds and lakes, and use partly submerged logs for basking. Yellow stripes on the head, neck and legs, and bright red patterns on shell.

The ideal home for a turtle is an indoor pond. This can be a large, wide, shallow fish-tank constructed from aquarium glass and held together with silicone rubber sealant. During the summer months, turtles may also live in an enclosed, escape-proof garden pond.

Young Painted Turtles are carnivorous. Feed turtle food and a variety of insect larvae, snails, worms and other pond creatures. Older turtles will eat fresh meat, lettuce and other salad vegetables. Provide vitamin supplements regularly.

Male Painted Turtles are smaller than the females. 2–20 oval eggs are laid from May to July in a deep, flask-shaped nest excavated by the female in soft soil. They will not hatch until the next summer and leave the nest only when conditions are warm enough.

Water Dragons (**1**) from SE Asia and Bearded Dragons (**2**) (20 in.) from Australia are tree-climbing forest dwellers. Water Dragons live near water and will escape into it if chased. In times of danger a Bearded Dragon puffs up its body and beard-like chin pouch.

Keep in a tall terrarium, at least 40 x 40 x 20 inches, heated to 82°F. Fit with branches and climbing indoor plants. Cover the floor with reptile substrate and provide a shallow bathing dish. Use a heating pad or spotlight to create a basking area at 104°F. Mist daily.

Dragon lizards eat live and wriggling insect prey every 2–3 days. Feed them large insects such as locusts, crickets, mealworms and household insects. Some may also take frozen baby rodents ("pinkies"), and pieces of fruit or salad leaves. Give multivitamins.

Following a lively courtship, the smaller female lays her eggs in a warm, moist nest. The young hatch several weeks later. Water and Bearded Dragons grow very quickly in captivity. They often reach maturity within 12 months.

GREEN ANOLE
8 inches

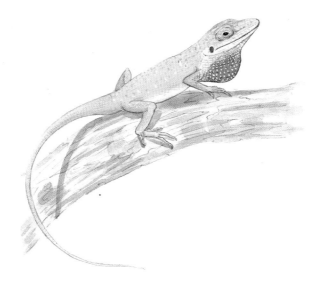

A small, slender lizard with a very long, thin tail. Found in the southeastern USA and the rain forests of Central America. Also called an American Chameleon because of its ability to change color from bright green to brown, depending on its mood.

Keep these tree-dwellers in a tall terrarium containing branches and climbing plants. Use a heat mat to provide background heating of 68°F. Provide a basking hot spot of 86°F by using a spotlight or heating pad. Cover the floor with rain forest substrate.

Feed live insects such as small locusts, crickets, mealworms, fruit flies, house flies and other domestic insects. Mist spray vegetation to increase humidity. Anoles will drink the drops of water that collect on leaves and will also sip drips of fruit purée and nectar.

Wild anoles live for 3 years. Keep one or more females with a single male – males will fight if kept together. Throughout the summer a female will lay a single egg in moist leaf litter once every 2 weeks. The young hatch after 5–7 weeks.

GREEN IGUANA
6½ feet

Live near rivers and ponds in the tropical forests of Central and South America. They are often found in trees, basking on a branch that overhangs the water. If danger threatens they drop into the water and swim away. A crest of spines extends to the tip of the tail.

Keep in a tall, heated terrarium fitted with a full-spectrum light and plenty of climbing branches. Handle regularly. Allow daily exercise – they love to climb furniture and take occasional swims in the bath. Can be kept outdoors in summer in a planted, aviary-like cage.

Adult Iguana eat a wide variety of plant foods such as grass, carrots, watercress, kale, turnip, parsley, lettuce and dandelion. Lentils, peas, beans and alfalfa sprouts provide protein. Young Iguana also eat mealworms and other insects. Give multivitamins.

Wild Iguana mate up to 90 days before the eggs are laid. The female lays 20–30 eggs in a long burrow in damp sand and protects the nest until the young hatch after 120 days. Young Iguanas are bright green. Pet animals rarely breed successfully.

CHAMELEONS

7–12½ inches *CAPE DWARF, HELMETED, JACKSON'S*

Cape Dwarf Chameleon (**1**) 7 in., from S. Africa, has a slightly raised casque (head crest). Helmeted Chameleon (**2**) 10 in., from E. Africa, has a tall rounded casque. The male Jackson's Chameleon (**3**) 12½ in., from E. Africa, has three small horns on its forehead.

Keep a single chameleon in a tall, ventilated terrarium, at least 24 x 30 x 20 inches, containing branches and climbing plants. Heat to 82°F during the day; reduce to 60°F at night. Mist for humidity at least twice a day. Difficult to keep; can easily become very stressed.

Feed a variety of insects every other day. Give grasshoppers, small locusts, crickets, cockroaches, houseflies and moths. They also take snails, slugs, and earthworms. Will drink the drops of water that form on plant leaves when the terrarium is misted.

Males nod and display to females before mating. Between 4 and 30 young are born 3–6 months later. Separate from the mother and rear the young individually. Feed fruit flies, small crickets and other tiny insects. The young become sexually mature at 9 months.

LEOPARD GECKO

12 inches

The Leopard Gecko lives in dry, rocky scrub from Iraq to northern India. It is one of the largest geckos and a popular pet. The skin is covered with small, granular scales and patterned with bands of buff and violet, dotted with bold, black spots.

Keep a pair in a dry, tall terrarium, at least 24 x 12 x 12 inches. Use a heating pad and a spotlight to maintain the temperature at 82°F during the day, but reduce to 60°F at night. Cover the floor with gravel substrate, and provide rocks to hide under and climb.

Feed crickets and a variety of other small insects. Food should be given in small quantities every other day. As with all captive reptiles, give a multivitamin supplement containing vitamins A, D and E twice a week. Water should be provided in a small shallow bowl.

After mating, the female lays two hard-shelled eggs, which she sticks to the sides of cracks and crevices in rocks, walls or tree bark. The eggs hatch in 8 weeks. In suitable conditions a single female will lay several clutches of eggs throughout the year.

CORN SNAKE
5 feet

Orange-gray with reddish-brown blotches and black spots, this
attractive snake is found in woodlands, fields and farm buildings
in southeastern and central USA. Captive-bred Corn Snakes
include several mutations – albino, red albino, black and striped.

Keep in a ventilated terrarium, 24 x 18 x 12 inches. Use a heating
pad, set low at 77–86°F; light for 8–10 hours a day. Line the tank
with compost, wood chips or savannah substrate. Provide branches
to climb, a bark, rock or log hideaway and a dish of water.

Wild Corn Snakes hunt mice and small birds. Pet snakes can be fed
entirely on frozen rodents obtained from pet shops. Feed newborn
"pinky" mice to young snakes and increase size of food as the snake
grows older. The mice must be completely thawed before eating.

Corn Snakes have lived for up to 21 years in captivity. They will
breed following winter hibernation – keep at 62–72°F for 3 months
and do not feed. Following courtship and mating, the female lays
4–30 eggs in damp soil, under cover. Incubate at 80–86°F.

COMMON GARTER SNAKE

2–4½ feet

The most common and widely distributed American snake. It is found throughout the USA (except the southwestern deserts) and southern Canada. It lives in meadows and marshes near water. Large numbers hibernate together in communal dens.

Active during the day along stream banks and meadows. Keep in a tank, 24 x 18 x 12 inches, with compost or rain forest substrate. Provide a bathing pool – a large, shallow terracotta dish is best, as it is easily cleaned. No need to heat if kept in a warm room.

Wild Garter Snakes eat frogs and tadpoles, as well as toads, salamanders, small fish, earthworms, snails and occasional mice. Pets snakes can be fed worms, caterpillars, snails (avoid garden slugs), fish and commercially produced Garter Snake food.

Garter Snakes live for 10 years. Easy to breed in captivity. Allow to hibernate over winter by placing in a cool, frost-free room. Following mating, the female gives birth to up to 85 young between June and October. Become sexually mature at 2 years.

⟨logo⟩ BOA CONSTRICTOR
1–18 feet

!

Boa Constrictors come from the rain forests of Central and South America. They should be considered as pets only if space for a terrarium several yards long and high can be provided. The cost of heating the terrarium and feeding these animals can be high.

House in a large, strong terrarium, heated to 79–84°F during the day (68–72°F at night), with a humidity of 80–90%. Provide peat or rain forest substrate, "forest" houseplants, such as fig, bromeliads, orchids and ferns, and strong branches for the snake to climb.

Captive Boas eat live mice, rats, small rabbits and chicks. Some can be coaxed to eat frozen rodents (after thawing) but many will refuse them. Provide bathing water in a large, heavy dish – the snakes will also use this as a toilet, so it should be cleaned regularly.

Boas can live for 30 years and grow rapidly. Following mating, 20–60 developed young are born. At birth they measure about 1 foot in length but by 12 months will have grown to 4 feet. Large Boas may bite other pets and small children.

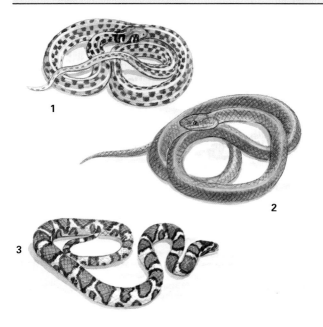

1

2

3

CHECKERED GARTER SNAKE (1) 3½ ft.
This snake comes from the arid
grasslands of southwestern USA.
Buff-colored with a brown,
checkered pattern along the
sides of the body. Give birth to
6–18 young. Keep in a dry
terrarium, provide rocks, bathing
dish and plant with cacti.

EUROPEAN RAT SNAKE (2) 6½ ft.
Also called the Aesculapian
Snake, it is found in central and
southern France, and ranges
eastwards to Turkey. It lives in
dry, rocky scrub and woodlands,
so pets can be kept in a dry,
unheated terrarium lined with
gravel. Furnish with stones,

rocks, logs or bark for cover and
branches to climb. Plant with
stonecrop, heather and herbs,
such as rosemary and thyme.
Feed frozen rodents (thawed).
The female lays 5–8 eggs, which
hatch within 60 days.

MILK SNAKE (3) 1–6½ ft.
A bright red snake, beautifully
patterned with black and white
bands,from central and eastern
USA. It closely resembles a coral
snake and, by mimicking this
poisonous species, it is avoided
by predators. King Snakes are
related to Milk Snakes, but are
mostly blackish-brown and
white in color.

113

GREEN TREE FROG

1¼–2½ inches

The American Green Tree Frog (illustrated) from the southern USA climbs in waterside foliage. A small, smooth-skinned frog, it can change its color from bright green to gray. At night, males make a far-carrying, quacking call. European Tree Frogs are similar.

Keep several frogs in a tall terrarium, 20 x 30 x 20 inches. Maintain temperatures at 80°F during the day, 68°F at night. Cover the floor with rain forest substrate or moist compost covered with moss. Provide climbing plants, branches and an upright log to climb on.

Will eat a variety of small, live garden insects and invertebrates such as flies, spiders, caterpillars, aphids, moths, and woodlice. Also give mealworms, fruit flies, small crickets and small locusts. Provide a large dish of water that should be changed daily.

Following hibernation (50°F for 2–3 winter months), breeding takes place at night in water. Males grasp the females around the middle; the eggs are laid in small, jelly-like masses. The bright green tadpoles remain in the water until metamorphosis at 2 months.

A large, fat, warty frog with a huge mouth and short legs. The eyes, protected by short fleshy horns, are located high on the head. They are often the only part of the frog visible when it burrows into leaf litter. Found in Argentina, Brazil and Uruguay.

Keep singly in a large tank, 24 x 18 x 18 inches, at 80°F. Fill with 8 inches (depth) of moist compost or rain forest substrate. Use moss, bark, dead leaves, ferns and pots of other "rain forest" plants to provide shelter. Add a large dish of water as a pool. Mist daily.

Wild frogs eat a variety of animals, from small mammals and birds to worms. Feed "pinky" mice, worms and snails to young frogs. Adults will take large mice and pieces of meat. Use long tweezers to give food or you may be bitten – this animal's gape is huge.

They mate in forest pools. The green tadpoles are patterned like their parents. As metamorphosis progresses, the back legs develop first, then the front legs and finally the tail is re-absorbed. Both the adults and the tadpoles are cannibals, so keep separately.

!

Oriental Fire-bellied Toads live in rivers, ponds, marshes and ditches in eastern Asia. A similar species is found in Europe and ranges into Asia. Both species have warty skin and a patterned, bright red and black underside.

Unlike most toads, these animals spend much of their time in water. Keep in a large aquarium divided into two sections by a waterproof partition, 8 inches high. Fill the larger section with water and aquatic plants. In the smaller part, fill with compost and plants.

Fire-bellied Toads float on the surface of the water, waiting for insects and other invertebrates. Feed crickets, mealworms, flies, grasshoppers, snails and worms. The skin of these toads secretes a toxic substance, so wear protective gloves when handling.

The male has a bell-like call, which he makes while resting at the pond surface. He clasps a female as she lays 40–100 eggs that stick to pondweeds. Remove spawn from the tank and raise separately in a tank of aerated pond water.

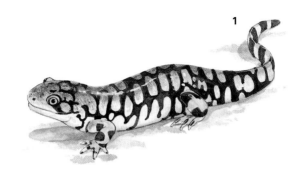

The Tiger Salamander (**1**) 13 inches, is the largest terrestrial amphibian. It is widespread throughout much of the USA. The brightly colored Fire Salamander (**2**) 10 inches, lives near water in mountain forests of central, western and southern Europe.

Keep a small pair (same species) in an unheated terrarium, 24 x 12 x 12 inches. Cover the floor with moist compost over a layer of gravel. Add rocks, fresh turf, some moss, bark, dead leaves, a rotting log and potted plants for cover. Provide a bowl for bathing.

Salamanders eat any live food that is small enough. Feed pets a variety of large insects such as crickets, locusts, mealworms and maggots, and also earthworms, slugs and snails. Large Tiger Salamanders will also take frozen mice (fully thawed, of course).

Use a breeding tank – half land, half water. Mating involves the exchange of a spermatophore between the sexes – on land in Fire Salamanders, or in water (Tigers) where the eggs are laid. Fire Salamanders bear developed young, which drop into the water.

AXOLOTL
10 inches

This is a Mexican salamander that keeps its aquatic lifestyle and larval shape, but is a sexually mature adult. The addition of iodine encourages an irreversible change to a terrestrial adult, gray with yellow spots. Albino, golden and pied mutations are available.

Keep in a 24 x 12 x 12 inches aquarium, filled with water to a depth of 8–12 inches. Line with gravel and an arrangement of rocks and aquatic plants. Aerate and filter the water, and maintain it at room temperature. Keep clean and change the water often.

A wild Axolotl eats any animal it can catch. Feed pets a variety of raw meats, including fish, and live food such as earthworms, snails, slugs, mealworms and crickets. Remove any uneaten food before it fouls the water.

Place a pair of Axolotls in a clean breeding tank. Add ice to reduce the water temperature (simulating meltwaters cooling the lake in spring). Courtship and spermatophore exchange follows. Eggs are laid onto water plants. Remove parents. The eggs hatch in 14 days.

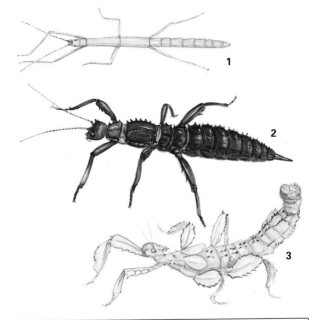

The hardy Indian Stick Insect (**1**) 4 inches, is harmless and an ideal beginner's pet. Larger species include the New Guinea "log" insect (**2**) 7¼ inches and the Australian "leafy" stick insect, known as Macleay's Specter (**3**) 6¼ inches, the males of which have wings.

About 20 Indian stick insects may be kept in a cage that is at least 18 inches tall, in a warm room. A glass-fronted insect cage with fine mesh sides is ideal. Propagators and fish tanks do not provide enough ventilation. Cover the floor with paper and replace weekly.

Stick insects eat fresh bramble leaves collected from hedgerows, parks and gardens. Avoid areas that have been sprayed. Indian stick insects also eat privet, ivy and the house plant *Maranta tricolor*. Place fresh sprigs in a jam jar of water or wet oasis block.

Indian Stick Insects live for a year. Most are female and do not mate. Adults continuously lay hard, brown eggs that fall to the floor. Save some to hatch 4 months later. The babies (nymphs) shed their skin six times in 5 months before reaching adulthood.

!

The docile, inexpensive Chilean Rose is a popular choice of tarantula. Buy only captive-bred specimens. Avoid handling and always wear gloves to avoid bites, which resemble a bee-sting. Irritating, itchy hairs, shed from the legs, cause skin rashes.

Keep a single tarantula in a small aquarium (10 x 8 x 8 inches) with a tight-fitting, ventilated lid. Fill with enough vermiculite, sand, gravel or savannah substrate, to burrow in, and add hollow rocks, bark or a half-buried clay flowerpot as cover. Maintain at 68–77°F.

Once a week, feed crickets, locusts and mealworms. Young spiders will take fruit flies and small worms. Provide a water dish containing a cotton pad to prevent drowning. A piece of buried hamster tube, open to the surface, makes an ideal hunting burrow.

The female weaves a nest of silk and hides inside it. She lays as many as 500 eggs in a silk cocoon and then wraps it up to make an egg sac. She will guard the nest until the eggs hatch. The spiderlings eat small insects such as fruit flies.

GIANT AFRICAN LAND SNAIL
4–12 inches

These huge snails from East Africa have been introduced to other parts of the tropics, where they have now become a serious pest. An easy pet to keep, inexpensive and cheap to feed. They will survive quite comfortably in a warm room.

Keep a single, small snail in a tank, 24 x 12 x 12 inches (larger if the snail grows very big), fitted with a secure, ventilated lid. Line the tank with paper, moist compost or gravel. Provide a shallow dish of water. Once a week empty the tank and clean thoroughly.

These snails eat any edible plant material. Feed a selection of kitchen fruit and vegetable trimmings such as cabbage, carrots, cucumber, tomato, salad leaves, potato and other roots. They will also eat dandelion, plantains and other wild plants.

They live for 5 years. Each animal is both male and female but they still need to mate. They breed readily, producing hundreds of offspring. 30–200 oval eggs are laid in damp soil and will hatch in 40 days at 77°F. Do **not** release them into the wild.

Glossary

albino – animal with no pigment in its skin or eyes, resulting in white fur or feathers and pink eyes.

carnivore – a meat-eating animal.

cere – fleshy, often colored swelling at the base of a bird's beak.

diarrhea – abnormally loose and fluid feces (droppings).

distemper – often fatal disease of dogs and ferrets.

domestic – tame animals that have been bred in captivity for a long time; often differ in appearance from their wild ancestors.

dorsal – on the back of an animal.

feline enteritis – inflammation of the stomach and intestine in cats, causing diarrhea and vomiting; usually fatal.

feline AIDS virus – an immune deficiency disease of cats.

hepatitis – disease of the liver.

hibernate – a deep winter sleep when the body metabolism and temperature drops; characteristic of many animals living in temperate regions.

infusoria – a food mixture of microscopic animals.

inoculate – treat with a mild dose of a particular disease to prevent, by immunity, further severe attacks of the same disease.

lagomorph – group of animals that includes rabbits and hares.

leptospirosis – often fatal disease of both animals and humans; can be caught from wild rat urine.

lutino – a yellow color variety in some birds.

mammary tumor – cancer of the breast.

metamorphosis – complete change of body form during development from larva to adult, as in amphibia.

mist – treat with a fine spray of water.

mongrel – crossbred animals whose parents are of different and often unknown breeds.

neuter – a male animal that has been castrated (that is, removal of the testicles).

parasitic worms – worms that live and feed within other animals, particularly in the gut.

parvo virus – causes bloody diarrhea in dogs; often fatal.

pedigree – pure bred animals whose ancestors are known, recorded and usually all belong to the same breed.

psittacosis – a disease of parrots and other birds that causes a serious type of pneumonia if transmitted to humans.

rabies – usually fatal disease that can be transmitted to humans from bites and scratches from infected mammals.

respiratory diseases – those that infect the lungs, nose and throat.

rodents – large group of mostly small mammals with gnawing teeth.

salmonella – bacteria that cause food poisoning in humans.

social – animals that would naturally live together in a group and would be unhappy if kept in a cage alone.

species – similar animals that can successfully breed with each other but not with other closely related species.

spermatophore – a packet of sperm transmitted from male to female during mating.

substrate – loose material used to cover the floor of a cage or terrarium; commercial products simulate natural habitats such as rainforest litter or desert sand.

Index